THE EXCITEMENT OF ANSWERED PRAYER

VIRGINIA WHITMAN

BAKER BOOK HOUSE
Grand Rapids, Michigan

CONTENTS

FISHHOOKS
TO FREIGHT CARS

We were trout fishing in a state park, using natural bait. My husband had gradually widened the distance between us as he waded downstream while I fished from the bank. Presently I landed a leaping, squirming beauty of a rainbow. After I threaded it on my stringer and went back to my line I discovered my steel hook was missing. Whether it had broken off in the fish, or what had happened, I could not tell.

"O Lord, what am I going to do?" I impulsively entreated. "I think I've used my last hook, and he's way off yonder."

Immediately after I finished praying, a gleam on the ground caught my eye. There at my feet lay a little brass hook the same size as the black one I'd lost!

"Thank you, Lord," I breathed as I tied it on my line.

The next day all the fishermen around me were catching trout on salmon eggs, which I did not have.

"Lord, I need some salmon eggs," I silently told my heavenly Father. I went on upstream and fished with artificial bait — unsuccessfully.

Returning to my original spot, I found that all the other fishermen had departed. Not a person was to be seen anywhere.

As I put down my gear, my eye caught sight of a discarded salmon egg jar. In it were all the eggs I had need of.

"Thank you, Father!" I exclaimed.

Such experiences make me grateful that there are no minimum or maximum limitations on prayer. One can pray about the most trivial items or the most consequential.

During the war, when materials were in shortage, we were building a cottage on the campus of a Bible school where we were going to live for a time and give our service. The cottage would become school property. Since the location was rural, on the shore of a large lake, it seemed that a rustic decor would be in order. We thought about making the interior walls of plasterboard which simulated knotty pine.

A Christian lumberman in a nearby metropolis was securing our supplies for us. When we consulted him about this type of plasterboard, he all but tore his hair over the idea of our thinking we might obtain such a commodity at that time.

"I don't know when there has been any of that available," he declared, "not for months and months. You'll have to plan something different."

"We're praying about it," we told him. "If it's the Lord's will, that is what we'd like to have."

In due time we heard from him. He was all but flabbergasted at what had happened.

"The railroad has notified me that I have a freightcar of lumber on the siding," he informed us by long distance call. "It's a carload of nothing but knotty pine plasterboard."

He had ordered it so long ago he had almost forgotten about it, or at least, had given up all expectation of ever receiving it. Together we rejoiced in God's goodness and in the fact that when it accords with his plan and purposes, he can arrange *anything* for his children. He is never before time, nor behind time, but always on time according to his schedule.

The variety of prayers that God answers is amazing. Just think of the many answered prayers of which we read in the Bible. Isaac prayed about Rebekah's failure to bear a child; David prayed for military counsel; Solomon prayed for administrative wisdom; Joel prayed about famine and drouth; Elijah prayed for rain; Jairus entreated for his daughter's healing; two blind men petitioned Jesus for sight; Philip asked for divine revelation; Paul prayed for survival in shipwreck; the early Christians prayed for Peter's release from prison and for guidance in matters of church policy.

Similar categories of prayer will be discussed later in these pages as proof that prayer is exciting because of the many areas of life in which it still operates in our times to link God's power with man's need.

God has plainly told us that we can ask for whatever we wish: "Don't worry about anything;

instead, pray about everything, and don't forget to thank him for his answers."[1]

In the King James Version, that verse ends with the words "let your requests be made known *unto God.*" That may sound absurd. To whom else would one pray?

Many prayers addressed to God, as far as the salutation is concerned, are nevertheless actually directed elsewhere in thought. A wife may be saying, "Dear God, please give my husband a raise in salary," but in her mind's eye is the image of the employer, and her hopes are actually toward him instead of God. That could account for a lack of assurance in prayer because one might be uncertain about a human person desiring to bless a fellowman. We can be sure, however, that God is willing, in fact, yearns to give his children all that he dares to. (There is always the danger of our becoming "spoiled brats" and he loves us too much to be party to that.)

When Peter was kept in prison by Herod it is recorded, ". . . but prayer was made without ceasing of the church unto God for him."[2]

Why would the Spirit have indited the phrase "unto God" in these two passages if it were not necessary to call attention to that aspect of prayer? As has been pointed out by various scholars, the biblical "formula" for prayer is unto God, in the Spirit,[3] using the name of Jesus Christ.[4]

Perhaps the word *formula* for prayer is unwise

---

[1]Philippians 4:6, *The Living Bible.*   [2]Acts 12:5.   [3]Ephesians 6:18.   [4]John 14:6, 14.

because it may convey or encourage mechanical mouthings, whereas prayer is not a ritual but a spontaneous communication which results in a transaction between God and the one who prays.

I like to say it this way: "You can do business with God through prayer."

That's one aspect that I find exciting — that I, an insignificant, clay individual with all the frailties of flesh, can have a transaction with the mighty God, Creator and Controller of the universe. Of course, and reasonably so, I must do business on his terms. I must meet the conditions of effective prayer which his wisdom has decreed.

The places where I am most apt to run counter to his conditions is in my motive and my goal. James, brother of our Lord, emphasized this when he wrote, "Ye ask, and receive not, because ye ask amiss, that ye may consume it upon your lusts"[5] [desires, cravings].

Commenting on this Scripture, George Müller said: "That is, persons who ask for things for the gratification of their carnal mind, that they may strengthen the old evil, corrupt nature in them — if they ask for that reason, then they ask amiss, and they have no warrant from Scripture to expect their prayers will be answered."

A great many prayers are selfishly conceived. They are offered predominantly with personal interests and ambitions in view. What can one do if he discerns that he has a selfish motive, though a proper goal? For example, a parent may pray

_____

[5]James 4:3.

for the regeneration of a lost son because his conduct is disgracing the family name, and not because he is misusing the fine body and personality with which God endowed him to serve for his glory.

The youth's salvation would be a proper prayer goal because the Bible assures us that God wants all men to be saved,[6] nevertheless the motive in praying for his salvation sprang, in this case, from selfish interests and desires.

The parent can confess his wrong motive[7] and ask God to purify it and make it a Spirit-begotten motive. Actually, all acceptable prayer is originally conceived by the Trinity and prompted by the Spirit. Ken Adams expresses that thought this way: "Prayer, as one of the vital functions of the church through each believer, is not that we bring to God some item of need which has come to our attention. Every item of need starts in the heart of God, finds its vocal expression through his body under the dictates of the Spirit and flows back to him — the Great Intercessor — who sits on the throne at the right hand of God, thus completing the cycle. That takes the strain out of praying, doesn't it, and turns it into a delight. It means that every time we pray we just join in on a prayer meeting that is already in progress!"[8]

Simon, the sorcerer of Samaria, is an example of one desiring a legitimate thing but with an illegitimate motive. According to the record, after

---

[6] 1 Timothy 2:4.   [7] 1 John 1:9.   [8]*International Viewpoint,* Nov. 1970.

seeing the miracles which God did through Peter and John by the Holy Ghost, he wanted the same gift, even to the point of offering to pay for it. Peter's rebuke was, ". . . your heart is not right before God."[9]

The same rebuke is deserved by many a child of God as he makes prayer requests of his heavenly Father. If we would pray effectively, we must constantly ask the Spirit to search our hearts, revealing our selfish motives to ourselves. We need the Spirit's help in bringing our prayers into conformity with God's plans for our prayer ministry.

A woman was invited to teach a Bible class in the absence of the regular teacher. She asked the Lord to guide her in her selection of material, method of presentation, and effort to stir to action in response to the passage being taught.

As she prayed and studied, she became aware, through the Spirit's conviction, that she had in the back of her mind a desire to surpass the teaching of other persons who sometimes substituted, and to draw the praise of the class members. In repentance she confessed her unworthy motive to God. She asked him to create in her a clean heart and renew a right spirit within her so that her motive in requesting help with the lesson would be purely for his glory. He did answer her prayer, she testified later, because when she stood to teach she never once thought about her presentation or what the reaction to it might be.

---

[9]Acts 8:21, TLB.

Her sole thought had been to communicate the message and the challenge of God's Word.

In view of incidents such as have been cited, what can you think of that is any more challenging than prayer? To be privileged to have a part in so extensive, so universal, so varied a ministry could surpass the discovery of a remedy for a formerly incurable disease. It could introduce more drama into a life than rescuing a trapped person from a burning building. Its outcome might top a rags-to-riches success story. It might provide more thrill than being crowned victor in an athletic event or queen in a beauty contest. It could result in more personal satisfaction than anything else that might occur in one's lifetime.

If you have missed such experiences through answered prayer, look into the matter. Examine the evidence in the pages which follow, ponder the possibilities, and resolve to meet the conditions so that you too can testify that answered *prayer is exciting!*

PREPARE
TO BE
ASTONISHED

A Christian couple purchased a new car. When they began to use it, they found that the heater did not work properly, which resulted in real discomfort to the wife. Without meaning to be unkind, the husband nevertheless very definitely refused to do anything about it.

"I'm not going to the trouble and uncertainty of having them monkey with it," he told her. "They would have to take out the radio, maybe would loosen up things that would make a rattle in the car, and perhaps result in other complications. It's all your imagination anyway," he dismissed the matter.

The wife saw no possible solution to her problem but she made it a subject of earnest prayer, asking God to undertake on her behalf and in some way solve her dilemma. In the meantime she threw a blanket over her lap when she entered the car, in order to keep the cold draft from aggravating arthritic pains.

Imagine her excitement when lightning struck the antenna of the car's radio, necessitating its removal for repair! In the course of that work the defect in the heater was discovered and corrected.

In answer to prayer, God sometimes arranges astonishing solutions to problems. Yet what we regard as astonishing might more often be classified as routine, were we willing to accept God at his word. Just think of some of the things which might be ours because God has promised them. Only because we so rarely claim his promises does what might be the ordinary seem extraordinary.

Past answers to prayer encourage us to expect astonishing things to happen. The Bible records some remarkable proof of this fact. Note these incidents:

Quail meat three feet deep — The Israelites in the wilderness, originally en route to the promised land of Canaan, tired of the heaven-sent manna, and grumbled loudly about it. Their ill humor, which might easily have erupted into a riot with the mob venting its anger on Moses for their predicament, prompted him to turn to God in prayer. He poured out his grievances, and asked the Lord what he was to do. He was so full of despair that he wanted to die.

God responded to Moses' appeal, gave him a plan to follow to obtain help in carrying his responsibilities, and promised the Israelites a month's supply of meat. Just how astonishing this answer was is evident when you consider there may have been over 600,000 persons to be fed.

The account of the provision is, "And there went forth a wind from the Lord, and brought quails from the sea, and let them fall by the camp . . . and as it were two cubits high upon the face of the earth."[1]

Strength to pull down a house — One of the best known characters of Bible times is Samson. Because we concentrate on this man's muscular miracles as well as his puttiness in the hands of a woman, his prayer power is sometimes overlooked. After God had seemingly abandoned him to the Philistines as penalty for his follies, Samson, blinded and ridiculed, called to the Lord, "O Lord God Jehovah, remember me again — please strengthen me one more time . . ."[2]

An entire army smitten with blindness — An incident in the life of the prophet Elisha involves two exciting answers to prayer. Elisha's life was threatened by the king of Syria who sent an army of horsemen and chariots to surround the city in which Elisha was tarrying. A young man who served the prophet, seized probably with both fear and dismay, cried out, "Alas, my master! what shall we do now?"

Elisha's response was to pray, "Lord . . . open his eyes and let him see." God did as requested and the young man saw "horses of fire and chariots of fire everywhere upon the mountain."

Then Elisha prayed regarding his enemies, "Lord, please make them blind." The prayer was answered, all were stricken blind, and Elisha was able to capitalize on the situation for his deliverance.[3]

Thousands of soldiers made corpses — Sen-

---

[1]Numbers 11.   [2]Judges 16:28, TLB.   [3]2 Kings 6, TLB.

nacherib, king of Assyria, railed on the kingdom of Judah, denied the deity of God, and purposed to conquer the nation. King Hezekiah of Judah cried out to God in desperation, and prayed, "O Lord our God, we plead with you to save us from his power; then all the kingdoms of the earth will know that you alone are God." (Note that he gave God's glory rather than physical preservation as his motive for requesting deliverance.)

God responded, for we are told, "That very night the angel of the Lord killed 185,000 Assyrian troops, and dead bodies were seen all across the landscape in the morning. Then King Sennacherib returned to Nineveh. . . ."[4]

A fish vomits out a man — Nearly everyone is familiar with some variation of the experiences of Jonah. Because of inaccurate reports (the Scripture does not say the fish was a whale) it is best to consult the Bible for the details. There we find that Jonah had been swallowed by a "great fish" and it was from its belly, with seaweed wrapped around his head, that Jonah recalled, "When I had lost all hope, I turned my thoughts once more to the Lord. And my earnest prayer went to you. . . ."

God heard Jonah's cry of distress and contrition. "And the Lord ordered the fish to spit up Jonah on the beach, and it did."[5]

What could be more astonishing than that?

Prison gates swing open — King Herod, reigning while Caesar was emperor of Rome, killed

---

[4]2 Kings 19, TLB.   [5]Jonah 1:15—2:10, TLB.

James and imprisoned Peter, probably hoping to curry favor with certain segments of the population. Intense prayer for the apostle's deliverance was offered by the local group of believers.

Relaxing in his trust in God, or his confidence in answered prayer, or both, Peter not only went to sleep in chains between two guards, but slept so soundly that the angel who came to escort him to freedom had to waken him with a firm whack on the side.

As they proceeded from the prison, it is recorded, "They passed the first and second cell blocks, and came to the iron gate to the street, and this opened to them of its own accord!"

An interesting sidelight on this astonishing answer to prayer is that when Peter reached the group who had been praying for him, they were too excited to believe it could really be he.[6]

Moreover, astonishing answers to prayer are not limited to Bible times. Contemporary Christians have many exciting experiences as a result of believing prayer. The requests and answers take in needs in every area of life. No doubt in each case the one involved was placing his faith in some Scripture pertinent to his need, so a related quotation has been included with each account. You may wish to make these passages your own, that you too can rely upon them in time of need.

Solace in suffering — A child of God became unable to stand or walk on her leg. The ailment

---

[6]Acts 12:1-16.

was diagnosed as an inflammation of the sciatic nerve. She was told that she would have to go to bed for a period of time. This was both inconvenient and expensive for her because it kept her from her work. She was reluctant to accept such a prescription, but was finally compelled to do so. She prayed much to the Lord about her trial.

Afterwards, looking back on the experience, she testified, "The thing that was precious to me in the ordeal was the sense of God's reality and presence, that he was right there with me as much as any human companion, fellowshiping with me in my misery, consoling me in my trial."

"He is like a father to us, tender and sympathetic to those who reverence him. For he knows we are but dust. . . ."[7]

Recovery from a virulent infection — An unsurrendered believer had frequently asked the Lord not to test her. She had indicated to him that though she was the recipient of salvation by grace through faith, she didn't want to undergo any trials such as bereavement, nor was she minded to commit herself to him to a degree that would result in anyone thinking she was at all fanatical.

Then she was seized with an acute form of kidney infection which was rarely successfully treated. The physician she consulted (a Jewish medical doctor) gave her that diagnosis and told her to set her house in order as he could give her

[7]Ps. 103:13, 14, TLB.

no assurance about the outcome, even though he would treat her in the best ways known to medical science.

Her condition worsened; eventually her body elimination was only pus and blood, and she was running a very high temperature. She came to the place of trying to bargain with the Lord. She told him that if he would heal her she would promise to witness to everyone with whom she came in contact as the Lord opened the way for her to do so.

Shortly afterwards she was able to eliminate in a normal manner, her fever left, and she recovered from her illness. She reported to her doctor, and upon examining her he asked what had happened.

"The Lord Jesus Christ healed me," she told him, whereupon he became very angry and declared, "That couldn't be."

She repeated her declaration, and he continued to discount it. He told her to return again at a certain date. She pointed out that there was no need to do so because she had been miraculously healed in answer to prayer. He took the position that there had merely been a remission and she would eventually have to return.

In testifying of the incident twenty years later, she explained that there never had been a recurrence of the ailment. Now, as a more mature Christian, she says that she would no longer try to strike a bargain with the Lord, but would simply pray and trust. Her case illustrates not only that God answers prayer for health in exciting ways, but also that he meets us on our prayer level, no matter how inexperienced we are.

"He nurses them when they are sick, and soothes their pains and worries."[8]

Fortitude in pain — A Christian discovered an abcess in her jaw. Consultation with her local dentist established that it was due to an impacted wisdom tooth. The X-rays were sent to a specialist in another city with a request for help. He returned them indicating that it required more delicate surgery than he wanted to undertake.

A second specialist to whom the X-rays were sent summoned the suffering woman in for a consultation. He explained that an important nerve lay along close to the tooth and that if he were to damage it during surgery she would be left without feeling in her jaw. If an anaesthetic were given, there would be no way of knowing when he was in contact with the nerve, with the possibility of damaging it. But if the operation were performed without anaesthesia, her reactions would be a barometer of his proximity to the nerve throughout the operation. He asked her if she thought she could endure such an ordeal.

She knew she couldn't in her own strength, but she felt that God would sustain her and give her courage to suffer the excruciating pain that would accompany such surgery. On a foundation of earnest prayer, the operation was successfully performed.

"Fear thou not; for I am with thee; be not dismayed; for I am thy God; I will strengthen thee;

8Ps. 41:3, TLB.

yea, I will help thee; yea, I will uphold thee with the right hand of my righteousness."[9]

Information supplied — A Christian journalist was walking back from the mailbox in a rural area when she saw an unusual creature crawling on the ground. It looked something like an overgrown centipede, yet had only four legs. The observer thought to herself that an account of it would be of interest to the readers of her natural history newspaper column if only she were sure what it was.

She tried to think of anyone who might correctly identify it for her. The conservation agent probably could, she recalled, but the county seat was twenty-five miles away and she didn't have time to go there.

"Lord, what can I do about it?" she prayed.

Later that afternoon a sudden and severe rainstorm blew up. It sent a boatload of men speeding to the columnist's covered dock for shelter. Her husband invited them in for coffee. Over it the couple learned that their guests were *all* conservation agents who were checking trot-lines in the area. God never does things by halves!

"Call unto me, and I will answer thee, and shew thee great and mighty things, which thou knowest not."[10]

A wasp immobilized — In a rural church a Bible teacher was preparing to teach a class of adult women who were seated in a section of the auditorium by a tier of open windows, there be-

---

[9]Isa. 41:10.   [10]Jer. 33:3.

ing no air-conditioning to combat the summer heat. Just as she introduced the lesson, a wasp came gliding in over the heads of the ladies. They began to duck and dodge and try to swat the feared insect. The teacher knew if that continued they would not hear the lesson nor derive any blessing from it, so she breathed a prayer to the Lord to take charge of the situation.

At the time, she was holding her open Bible in her left hand. Almost immediately the wasp lit on the top part of the binding which hangs loose from the back when the book is open. The ladies began to point to it.

"That's all right," the teacher said. "Just forget about it. I'm not afraid of it and the Lord will take care of the matter."

The insect stayed right there through the entire period. Just as she closed the lesson, the wasp lifted its wings and disappeared out the window. Haven't we a wonderful God?

"Yes, ask *anything,* using my name, and I will do it."[11]

Weather tempered — A kindergarten teacher in a large city was scheduled to take her pupils to the zoo. She prayed for favorable weather because it would expedite arrangements and make the occasion more enjoyable. The day of the trip was the only day that week that it did not rain.

"Elijah was as completely human as we are, and yet when he prayed earnestly that no rain

---

[11]Jn. 14:14, TLB.

would fall, none fell for the next three and one half years."[12]

Handicap overcome — Following two falls on ice as a girl, a sixty-five-year-old Christian woman had become crippled and could walk only bent over with the upper half of her body horizontal. She had been that way for eighteen years, having been in the hospital twice in traction, and having been treated unsuccessfully in other ways.

Finally, a group of believers went to her home, gave her Scripture, encircled her and laid hands on her while a pastor led in prayer. Then he took her by the hand and said, "In the name of Jesus, stand up."

She stood up straight and continued to walk erectly thereafter, radiant over God's answer to prayer.

". . . they shall lay hands on the sick, and they shall recover."[13]

Heartbeat restored — A missionary on a foreign field was dealing with an inquirer when a servant came and tried to speak to him. The minister felt that nothing could be as important as leading a man to Christ, so he ignored the national. The servant persisted, and finally got through to his master with his message: "Your little daughter's throat has been slashed by a dog."

The missionary ran home to find a maid holding the inert body of his five-year old girl. She had been attacked when she tried to protect her younger sister from the animal. The man gath-

---

[12]Jas. 5:17, TLB.   [13]Mk. 16:18.

ered the child into his arms and ran for the mission hospital, praying that the doctor would be there, although ordinarily he was not on duty at that hour.

The physician was there, but when he examined the child he announced that he could detect no heartbeat. The father flung himself over the little girl, broken-heartedly importuning God to undertake on her behalf. Suddenly she said, "Hello, Daddy." The doctor gave her a blood transfusion, and before long she was back to normal.

"And the prayer of faith shall save the sick, and the Lord shall raise him up . . ."[14]

The same missionary was waiting outside the delivery room as his wife gave birth to another child. The doctor rushed out and cried, "Pray! Your wife is having a heart attack." The husband immediately fell to his knees. God gave him assurance that the mother would be spared. He afterward explained, "I felt as if I were sitting in a love seat with Jesus," and the wife testified that she had had the same assurance.

"Don't worry about anything; instead, pray about everything; tell God your needs and don't forget to thank him for his answers. If you do this you will experience God's peace, which is far more wonderful than the human mind can understand. His peace will keep your thoughts and your hearts quiet and at rest as you trust in Christ Jesus."[15]

On another occasion the family were all suffer-

---

[14]Jas.5:15.   [15]Phil. 4:6, 7, TLB.

ing from colds when the weather turned extremely chilly. They were without fuel, so after prayer the man went out to see if he could find any wood to burn. He came back empty handed. To his amazement, he found his bin full of coal. No one knew where it came from. Even his "nosy" neighbor, who never seemed to miss a single thing that went on, said he had seen no one come or go.

"But my God shall supply all your need according to his riches in glory by Christ Jesus."[16]

Reprieve from death and hell — As a result of a severe storm, an operator in a power plant was instructed to go find the places where lines were down and report them. The man left on the assignment, accompanied by his brother-in-law and another man.

In the course of his inspection the employee came in contact with a 2300-volt bare copper line direct from bus bars at the generating plant. The then non-Christian man relates that in the split second before he was knocked down, blinded, deafened, rendered speechless, and burned, he cried to God, "O Lord, forgive me every sin I ever committed and save my soul."

His brother-in-law immediately began giving the unconscious man artificial respiration while the third man went for help. It is reported that it was at least twenty minutes before the doctor arrived, during all of which time artificial respiration was given without response.

---

[16]Phil. 4:19.

The doctor examined the man, pronounced him dead, and had a sheet thrown over him preparatory to the body being taken to the morgue by an ambulance which had arrived.

The brother-in-law thrust aside the sheet and frantically resumed artificial respiration. Suddenly the victim commenced to bleed from ears, nose, and mouth, and he tells that he himself heard someone say, "Get this man to the hospital before he bleeds to death."

He points out that had he been conscious before that time, he would have previously bled, and that in the ordinary course of events, one without blood would have suffered brain damage. He also reports that he at that time had a vision of the lake of fire and the total darkness which is the lot of the unbeliever. In due time he was completely healed with all his faculties functioning normally. He became a minister of the gospel and the first person he led to Christ was the doctor who had pronounced him dead.

"And it shall come to pass, that whosoever shall call on the name of the Lord shall be saved."[17]

What was the common denominator of all these incidents? Wasn't it a problem that man could not solve himself, and a turning to a God who was abundantly able to cope with it? We call it prayer, and isn't it exciting?

---

[17]Acts 2:21.

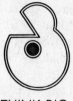

THINK BIG

A missionary in South America was driving through southern Mexico accompanied by his wife. Map in hand, she was serving as navigator, but with difficulties.

"It's too bad we don't have a Texaco map of Central America," her husband told her. "They are always so good."

At that moment the wind blew the speaker's cap from his head, and he had to stop the car and walk back to retrieve it. As he was returning to the car he saw a piece of paper down the road ahead so he walked on to pick it up. It was a brand new Texaco map of the area![1]

This incident was viewed by the couple as an illustration of Isaiah 65:24: "And it shall come to pass, that before they call, I will answer; and while they are yet speaking, I will hear."

It was also a heart-warming illustration of Ephesians 3:20: "Now unto him that is able to do exceeding abundantly above all that we ask or think, according to the power that worketh in us. . . ."

---

[1]Reported in *Brown Gold*, July 1970.

God is more than willing for us to pray with great expectations. He has even spelled it out for us by telling us that when we need a mountain moved we don't have to have a steam shovel, bulldozer, or other expensive equipment along with skilled operators. All we need is faith in him, his power, and his willingness.

The Bible encourages us to think big about *situations*. Hannah was barren. Her husband's other wife taunted her about it. Naturally, Hannah was grieved and frustrated by her trial. Neither husband nor doctor (had one been available) could remedy the matter. Only God could alter her plight. It was to him that she went in her bitterness of soul. He heard her prayer and removed her barrenness. Subsequently she conceived and bore, first Samuel, and then other children.[2]

No situation is too desperate for God to remedy in answer to scriptural prayer.

The Bible also encourages big expectations about *resources*. Scripture records a time during the ministry of Elisha when the Syrians were seeking to destroy the Israelites. Ben-hadad mustered the Syrian army and besieged Samaria. The siege was so long and intense that food supplies in the city were exhausted, and famine prevailed.

Evidently Elisha had been praying about the scarcity of food stuffs and its accompanying inflation, because God instructed him to tell the people that on the next day food would be avail-

---

[2]1 Sam. 1:1—2:21.

able at noninflationary prices. (One man was so blasphemous in his doubt of this promise that he suffered death as a consequence.) True to Elisha's prediction, plenty was provided within a matter of hours.[3]

Resources are always available for God's use in answering scriptural prayer. Many a pastor can recall proof of that very fact. For example, one preacher gives this testimony: "When my wife and I were still living in a seminary apartment, and I was in the last month of study before graduation, we were facing serious financial problems. At the time, I was pastor of a small church in Louisiana. They were paying me $35 per week. Needless to say, it was difficult to buy gasoline for the one-hundred-sixty-mile round trip to our church field twice a week on this amount. With graduation only two weeks away, we still owed the seminary $50. Since the seminary had a ruling that all bills had to be paid before graduation, we were somewhat apprehensive. We decided to take the matter to the Lord in prayer, but confess that we did not expect an answer so soon nor so exact. On the day that we began to pray, we discovered a note in our mailbox telling us that an anonymous person had deposited $50 in our account in the business office. To this day, I do not know the name of the benefactor; actually it was God."

Furthermore, the Bible encourages big expectations about *circumstances*. For instance, Joshua

---

[3] 2 Kings 6, 7.

was once sent an urgent message to come help the Gibeonites because the Amorites were about to conquer them. Joshua evidently talked to the Lord while he marched to their assistance because God assured him of his intervention. During the ensuing battle God did in fact slay more invaders with mammoth hailstones than the Israelites killed with the sword. However, darkness was approaching and Israel's victory was not yet complete, so Joshua prayed God to make the sun stand still until the battle could be won. God answered his prayer.[4]

In later years King Jehosaphat of Judah found the nation in a difficult set of circumstances which he reviewed before the Lord in prayer. He reminded God of how he had not permitted the children of Israel, en route to the promised land, to overrun the Amorites, Moabites, and Edomites, Now, he reported, these very people were about to drive out the Israelites. He told God they didn't know what to do in such circumstances, but he said, ". . . our eyes are upon thee."

With noteworthy faith, the nation, under Jehosaphat's leadership, began to praise God for what he would do, and their expectations were fulfilled. God set the factions to warring with each other before they ever reached a place of battling the forces of Judah. They destroyed one another, and this provided immense spoil for Jehosaphat and his warriors.[5]

There will never be a set of circumstances that

---

[4]Joshua 10.   [5]2 Chron. 20.

God cannot manipulate so as to answer scriptural prayer. A senior citizen reports this example of such an experience: "Our old car would no longer pass inspection. In our mid-seventies, and living on Social Security, we had no funds for another car. We could not stay in our pleasant but isolated home in the country without transportation. Uncertainty existed on our part, but God knew the answer. An old friend had died recently, leaving me a legacy, but I had no idea whether it would be substantial, nor did I expect the estate to be settled promptly enough to be of help in this crisis. Then came the news that bequests were to be paid soon. The amount would be enough to buy a second-hand car about six years old.

"God led us to the car, one with low mileage. Despite small delays and some uncertainties, in God's accurate timing we took possession and could travel once more. Some would call this a coincidence, but I have had too many of these 'coincidences' in my prayer life to fail to see the hand of God in the way things happen."

A pastor had an impression that perhaps the church he served should start a bus ministry. He asked the Lord to lead. Not long after, he mentioned it to one of his deacons, who was a car dealer. The man was only lukewarm in his interest because he was aware of the many angles to be considered, such as liability insurance, maintenance, etc.

Soon after that, a customer brought in a bus to trade on a new car. It had no seats in it because it had been fitted up as a camping unit. Therefore the dealer did not give much thought to the matter of what the pastor had said.

A week or so later another man came in and looked at the bus. He explained that he already had a bus but would like to trade the dealer the seats from it for the camping equipment. Then the dealer concluded that the Lord was involved and was presenting an opportunity. Imagine the rejoicing when the church was informed of what had transpired and was made a gift of the bus.

There is also encouragement to great expectations of answered prayer in specific areas.

To illustrate, an African boy had heard a Bible story that encouraged him to trust God for physical safety. This eleven-year-old lad and his mother, both Christians, walked four miles to a chapel for Sunday worship and instruction. Their route lay through thick bushes where many wild animals lived. The boy carried a spear over his shoulder, but in many months of traversing the jungle had never had occasion to use it.

Early one morning, however, a lion emerged from a thicket and jumped at the boy before he had opportunity to climb a tree as his mother did. He threw his spear, striking the lion's eye, but not killing the roaring beast. This turned it aside and gave the boy time to climb a tree out of its path. For an hour the lion thrashed around trying unsuccessfully to dislodge the spear. Finally the beast bounded away. After a proper lapse of time the mother and son descended and continued their trek to the chapel, arriving just as the service terminated.

When his friends at the chapel heard the story they found it hard to believe. The following week they made it a point to check it out and discovered the lion's tracks and then its carcass, with the boy's spear still in it. The next Sunday the men asked the youth how he had strength and courage for his feat.

He replied that he had neither, but had heard the story of Daniel in the lions' den and had resolved that if he ever encountered a lion he would call upon Daniel's God for help. He said that when the lion jumped at him he shouted, "Lord Jesus, shut that lion's mouth!"

He went on to testify, "Then I threw my spear. I knew I could not do it myself. I believe Jesus heard my prayer, guided the spear for me, and saved our lives."[6]

Another area in which we must think big is that of wisdom and guidance. For that, there is this assurance: "If you want to know what God wants you to do, ask him, and he will gladly tell you, for he is always ready to give a bountiful supply of wisdom to all who ask him; he will not resent it. But when you ask him, be sure that you really expect him to tell you, for a doubtful mind will be as unsettled as a wave of the sea that is driven and tossed by the wind. . . ."[7]

An elementary school teacher contracted to teach a first grade which she understood would consist of fifteen pupils. She discovered at the

---

last moment that the room was not in readiness, that no supplies had been ordered, and that the enrollment was nearly double what she had been led to expect. It was a dismaying situation.

God, however, had not been taken by surprise. He sent to the school that opening day two mothers, themselves once pupils of this teacher, and they stayed throughout the morning, assisting her in handling the children. The teacher knew that this unexpected aid had appeared in answer to her prayers and those of others who had covenanted to pray for her on that morning.

"I will instruct thee and teach thee in the way which thou shalt go; I will guide thee with mine eye."[8] Such a promise was believed by a native Christian in Brazil. Though he was advanced in years and rich only in faith in God, he traveled the Amazon river by canoe, bearing the good news of the gospel to the tribes who dwelt on its banks. He testified, "I never know where it is that God wants me to stop and preach so I pray, 'Lord, as I paddle down this river, if you have someone to whom I must go with your saving word, let it rain just as I am passing their house. I will stop and share the good news.' Many times," he said, "an entire family has accepted Christ when God led me by his rain."[9]

In Spain a woman had come from the village of LaMancha to the city of Madrid to be with her brother who was ill. Being an evangelical, she was anxious to locate a church of that type.

---

[8]Ps. 32:8.   [9]Quoted from February 1971 *Commission*.

Not being able to learn of one, she asked God to guide her. She told him she would take a bus to the center of town and expect him to do the rest. Her family said she was crazy to go looking for a small church in a city of three million people, especially when she herself was blind.

Nevertheless, the woman boarded the bus with faith in God to direct her. Soon another woman got on and sat down beside her. The evangelical gave the newcomer a tract whereupon the recipient asked where she got it. In the conversation which followed, the Madrid resident mentioned that she was going to church.

"Could you tell me where the First Baptist Church is located?" the blind woman asked.

"That's where I am going," the other woman replied. "You can go along with me."[10]

Such experiences are proof that one can assuredly have great expectations of answered prayer. Faith is the decisive factor. "Listen to me! You can pray for anything, and if you believe, you have it; it's yours!"[11]

The Bible defines faith as follows: "Now faith is the substance of things hoped for, the evidence of things not seen."[12]

Jesus spoke of degrees of faith:

No faith — "And he said unto them, Why are ye so fearful? how is it that ye have no faith?"[13]

Little faith — "And if God cares so wonder-

---

[10]Reported in *Word and Way*, Jan. 7, 1971.   [11]Mk. 11:24, TLB.
[12]Heb. 11:1.   [13]Mk. 4:40.

fully for flowers that are here today and gone tomorrow, won't he more surely care for you, O men of little faith?"[14]

Great faith — "When Jesus heard these things he marveled at him, and turned him about, and said unto the people that followed him, I say unto you, I have not found so great faith, no, not in Israel."[15]

Study of the context seems to indicate that those of little faith had their eyes on the problem and the odds against its solution. Those of great faith had their eyes on Jesus, the Problem Solver. The incident of Peter attempting to walk on the water supports this theory. As long as his eyes were on Jesus he was buoyed up, but when he got his eyes on the water he began to sink. He had enough faith to call on Jesus to save him but Jesus evaluated his faith as "little" in degree.

Faith, of course, is not a quantity that can be measured with a quart cup or a bushel basket. The effectiveness lies in its virility, not its volume. This might be illustrated by comparing dry cell and transistor batteries. The latter are smaller in size but mightier in power. Jesus said faith as a grain of mustard seed could be powerful enough to move a mountain.

Viewing the problem as more real and present than the Solver is what constitutes doubt. Doubt paralyzes and renders inactive. It may be helpful here to stop and think about how we feel when someone doubts our word. We are apt to consider it an insult, and view it as tantamount to calling us a liar. How, then, does our doubt seem to God?

Jesus pointed to doubt as the reason the disciples could not relieve the demon-possessed boy.[16] Prayer, to be effective, must be vitalized by faith. "You can get anything — *anything* you ask for in prayer — if you believe."[17]

That the father of the demon-possessed youth recognized this fact is evidenced by his response when Jesus said, "Anything is possible if you have faith." To which the man replied, "I *do* have faith; oh, help me to have more."[18]

It is plainly stated, "You can never please God without faith, without depending on him. Anyone who wants to come to God must believe that there is a God and that he rewards those who sincerely look for him."[19]

How is one to acquire faith if his is weak or lacking? Paul supplied a clue: "So then faith cometh by hearing, and hearing by the word of God."[20]

Studying the Bible so that one becomes familiar with the experiences recorded there, and so that he has a working knowledge of God's promises and assurances, is a sure way of converting *no* faith or *little* faith to *great* faith.

For instance, one may be undergoing severe trial. He recalls how God delivered David from his enemies or Peter from prison. It encourages him to trust God to see him through his difficulties.

---

[16]Mt. 17:20.   [17]Matt. 21:22, TLB.   [18]Mk. 9:23, 24, TLB.
[19]Heb. 11:6, TLB.   [20]Rom. 10:17.

Or he remembers one of God's promises such as, "When you go through deep waters and great trouble, I will be with you. When you go through rivers of difficulty, you will not drown! When you walk through the fire of oppression, you will not be burned up — the flames will not consume you."[21] As he thinks on the promises of God he is enabled to believe that God will maintain him.

Another means of receiving or augmenting faith is by prayer. "And the apostles said unto the Lord, increase our faith."[22] We, too, may ask God to impart faith to us or to strengthen what little we have to the degree of expecting great things from him in answer to prayer. Let us keep in mind the rebuke of James: ". . . The reason you don't have what you want is that you don't ask God for it,"[23] and as we have need of it let us ask for increased faith.

A college-age Christian youth was about to leave home for the first time to take a summer job several states away. His mother was concerned for both his physical safety and spiritual welfare, and prayed much about it.

In due time he arrived safely at his destination and wrote back that his new employer was a Sunday school teacher who had invited him to church the first Sunday he was there. The mother was fervently thankful to God for the way in which her prayers had been answered and the answer served to give her assurance that had been lacking. It built up her faith.

---

[21]Isa. 43:2, TLB.　　[22]Lu. 17:5.　　[23]Jas. 4:2.

Faith is the bucket we let down by prayer's rope into the well of God's abundance. What we bring up depends upon what we let down. We have every encouragement to use a big bucket.

STIRRING EXAMPLES
FROM CHRIST'S LIFE

Christ never experienced an emergency. Because of his divine foreknowledge he was always prepared for any incident. The fact, however, does not rob any of his encounters with problem-plagued people of excitement for the person involved.

Very little imagination is required to visualize the excitement of persons favored by Jesus' answer to their prayer. (We use the term prayer here in its wider sense of communion with Jesus about one's needs.) Take, for example, the leper who prayed, "If you want to, you can make me well again."[1] He had been compelled to dwell by himself; if any other human being approached him he had to cry out, "Unclean! Unclean!"

In the initial stages of his affliction the leper no doubt experienced tingle and pain, then numbness of tissue, and finally the loss of flesh and faculties. Along with those distressing symptoms had been the alienation from his family and fellowmen for no telling how long. What loneliness, heartache, and despair must have been his!

---

[1]Mk. 1:40-45, **TLB**.

Then came hope. Perhaps from a distance he had witnessed other healings. Faith sprouted! He developed assurance that Christ could heal him, and he sought opportunity to make request. The obstacle that loomed the largest in his sight, "if you want to," did not exist, because Christ was not only willing but anxious for the leper to be made whole.

Notice the word that pictures his excitement over answered prayer after his contact with Christ. He began to *shout* the news of his healing. He was consumed with eagerness to tell what had happened to him. In contrast, do we disappoint God by our failure to be excited about answered prayer?

Or think of the excitement of various parents who had prayers for their children answered. Jairus asked Jesus to come and lay hands on his ailing daughter but she had died by the time they reached her. What dismay must have been the father's, and then what heart-bursting joy as Jesus raised her from the dead![2]

The Syro-Phoenician woman begged Jesus to help her demented daughter[3] and a man made request for his deranged or epileptic son.[4] Both had their prayers answered. After perhaps years of frustration, embarrassment, and discouragement their whole life pattern must have been altered from one of custodial responsibility to encouraging expectation of normal development. Can you imagine the emotions in each instance?

---

[2]Mk. 5:22-43. [3]Matt. 15:21-28. [4]Lu. 9:37-43.

Or picture the cases of the blind and the deaf, the lame and the paralyzed. What excitement must have attended each as despair was turned to hope, disability to capability, a passive existence to an active one.

It we can but recognize it, there is an excitement potential in the prayers Jesus prayed which are being answered in our day. Christ petitioned God thus: "I am not praying for these alone [i.e. the apostles] but also for the future believers who will come to me because of the testimony of these."[5] That means you and me and our fellow Christians!

Did you see a victory in the life of a hard-pressed brother in Christ? It may have been an answer to this prayer Jesus had offered even before Calvary. Did you see a miraculous deliverance from danger? A healing with or without medical aid? A favorable manipulation of circumstances? An unexpected resolution of problems? Think about the centuries of time since Jesus anticipated the need and prayed about it. Isn't that exciting?

With such thoughts can come the realization that we were in view when Christ prayed for the Holy Spirit's presence with believers[6] and for their deliverance from evil[7] as well as for their ultimate translation into glory.[8] What could be more exciting than all which is involved in the answers to these prayers of his? Additional excitement is afforded by the thought of his present

---

[5]Jn. 17:20, TLB.   [6]Jn. 14:16.   [7]Jn. 17:15.   [8]Jn. 17:24.

intercession for us at the right hand of God.[9]

Moreover, awesome excitement may be aroused by the contemplation of how Jesus' prayers for himself were answered. He begged God, "Father glorify thy name," and the answer came from God, "I have both glorified it, and will glorify it again."[10] And he did glorify it in his Son's sacrificial death, his triumphant resurrection from the grave, and his predicted ascension into heaven. He will yet glorify it further in his rapturous return for the saints, his millennial reign, and his final revelation with the new heaven and new earth. Hallelujah! That's exciting to think about!

What is the key to Christ's exemplary prayer life? "I do always the things that please him."[11] "My nourishment comes from doing the will of God who sent me. . ."[12]

Thus it will be for us. Our prayers will be answered as we obey his wishes and abide in his will. Those are the factors that guarantee exciting answers to prayer.

"And whatsoever we ask, we receive of him because we keep his commandments and do those things which are pleasing in his sight."[13] "If you stay in me and obey my commands, you may ask any request you like, and it will be granted."[14]

A lovely Christian wife, mother of teen-age children, blacked out unexpectedly and unexplainably. As a result of hospital tests, a tumor was

---

[9]Heb. 7:25; 12:2.   [10]Jn. 12:28.   [11]Jn. 8:29.   [12]Jn. 4:34.
[13]1 Jn. 3:22.   [14]Jn. 15:7, TLB.

discovered on her brain. In surgery it was found that all of it could not be removed without loss of her life. She was given less than a year to live.

After a remarkable restoration to activity where she travels, attends meetings, and performs some of a homemaker's tasks, she writes, "Talk about answered prayer, believe me I am one . . . I was at the doctor's again a week ago and he was so happy with me. After my operation he was sure if I lived for five or six months that would be a long time. Here it is a year and a half. . . ."

What is the background of this exciting prayer answer for those who love and esteem this child of God? Statements such as these reveal her desire to obey and abide: "I know my Lord has a purpose for this . . . Please pray with me that my Lord can use me whether it be a day or years, with nothing in mind but his glory."

A Christian writer had a cookbook published. She prayed that she would have a satisfactory sale on the edition. The good Lord arranged a surprise for her of which she had not dreamed. She was invited to go to another country, demonstrate her cookery, and lecture about it. All expenses were paid, and she received a generous honorarium besides. She testified, "I am just stunned by the miracle part of it. Here I was praying, and got so much more than I was praying for, but that is the way it always works out. I just want to do what I can in every detail for the glory of God. . . ."

Along with obedience as a condition for praying with assurance is another quality which Jesus exemplified; a fervent desire, a spirit of earnestness. This is evidenced in the statement, "While Christ was here on earth he pleaded with God, praying with tears and agony of soul. . . ."[15]

How long has it been since you wanted something so passionately that you wept about it as you prayed? Our lukewarm prayers must often, as one forthright person expressed it, "make God sick to his stomach."

Closely related to earnestness in prayer is perseverance in prayer. Jesus related a parable on this subject.[16] Many of our desires are so spasmodic and superficial that we often do not remember a week later that we prayed urgently about them.

This is not to imply that repetition is necessary in order to jog God's memory or wear down his resistance, but it may very well be an index to the depth of our concern and the earnestness of our prayer.

Christians in a foreign country were anxiously seeking a location for a chapel, but no one would rent to them for fear of arousing hostility. There was a vacant church (with a small auxiliary building beside it) which seemed ideal for their need. It had been built by a wealthy business man, a national who had incurred ill-will and was not permitted by the government to open it after he had built it. Nevertheless, the man refused to rent it to the evangelicals.

The group seeking a church building kept looking elsewhere. One of the missionaries, however,

---

[15]Heb. 5:7, TLB.   [16]Lu. 18:1-8.

was so impressed that this was exactly what was needed that she continued steadfast in prayer that it might become available to them.

Meanwhile, the Christians were permitted to use a police hall, and they thought that eventually they would be able to secure it on a permanent basis. Instead, its use was withdrawn. The group felt frustrated, but the one missionary kept on praying for the property she thought ideal. In the interval that had elapsed, the building had been sealed by the government because it had been illegally used. Imagine the surprise and delight of the Christian group to have the minister of Protestant affairs approach them and *ask* them to use the building in order to resolve a controversial situation. The missionary's perseverance in prayer had been honored by God!

Obedience, earnestness, and perseverance have been cited as conditions of effectual prayer. Have any of your prayers been hindered by lack of these qualities? If you were issued a report card grading you on them, how would it read? If your rating would be poor, don't be dismayed or disheartened; talk to God about it. Ask him to give you the spirit of prayer that Jesus had.

Remember that there is no situation or geographic location where prayer cannot operate, no problem so complicated or anguish so deep that prayer cannot penetrate, no condition so irremediable that prayer cannot alter it. "For with God, nothing shall be impossible."[17]

---

[17]Lu. 1:37.

THE SPIRIT
OF LIVELY HOPE

A real spirit of prayer pervaded a convention held in Nagaland, India. Contributing to the prayerful atmosphere was the Christian background of the whole region where all the state government officials were Christians and where all government meetings were opened with prayer.

A featured speaker at the convention reported, "Seldom have I felt the presence of God as we did . . . There was an overwhelming consciousness of his presence . . . There was a small thatched auxiliary building where prayer was offered around the clock. I stepped into this room several times during the convention, and each time I sensed power, although you couldn't hear anything. The only similar experience I can relate it to is when I stood on top of a turbine at a TVA dam. I could feel the surge of power though I couldn't hear anything. I got the same feeling standing in that tiny prayer room."[1]

There are no exciting answers to prayer without the attendant ministry of the Holy Spirit. One becomes indwelt by him when he receives Christ

[1]World Vision *Heartline*, June 1971.

as his personal Savior, his atoning sin-bearer. One may, however, request the Holy Spirit in prayer.

Some Bible scholars interpret the statement, "If ye then, being evil, know how to give good gifts unto your children: how much more shall your heavenly Father give the Holy Spirit to them that ask him?"[2] to mean not the indwelling Spirit, but the spirit of prayer. In his book *Prayer,* O. Hallesby has a helpful chapter devoted to the subject "The Spirit of Prayer" and earnestly advocates praying for it.

John Fletcher, a before-our-time saint, prayed thus: "Give me thy abiding Spirit, that he may continually shed abroad thy love in my soul. Come, O Lord, with that blessed Spirit! Come thou and thy Father in that holy Comforter. . . . pour out thy Spirit; shed him abundantly on me, till the fountain of living waters abundantly springs up in my soul. . . ."

Whatever the exact significance of Luke's passage on praying for the Holy Spirit, it can do no violence to it for one to pray for the Spirit of prayer. When the heart is cold and indifferent or the mind cluttered and self-concerned, certainly then is the time to pray for the Spirit of prayer to be kindled within. The chorus "Spirit of the Living God, Breathe on Me" is an excellent prayer-hymn for such a situation.

Paul admonished, "Praying always with all prayer and supplication in the Spirit . . ."[3]

---

[2]Lu. 11:13.   [3]Eph. 6:18.

Jude exhorted, "But ye, beloved, building up yourselves on your most holy faith, praying in the Holy Ghost . . ."[4]

One may ask, "What does praying in the Spirit involve?"

It means that one is neither grieving[5] nor quenching[6] the Spirit. (Someone has pointed out that saying no to God quenches the Spirit and saying yes to Satan grieves him.) It means being surrendered to the· Spirit's control and looking to him for guidance as to what to pray for.

Christians have been known to be impressed to pray about a given matter or for a particular person without knowing any special reason for doing so. Subsequent events have corroborated the fact that they were praying in the Spirit, that is, that the Spirit had prompted them to pray as they did.

Five men in a Christian tour group had flown ahead to Cairo, Egypt. As they were landing there one of the men had a mental image of a plane in trouble over the ocean. He interpreted it as involving those who had been left behind for a later embarkation. So grave was his apprehension that he asked the other four to pray, because he knew there was an emergency.

The next day they learned that as the others were taking off from Athens their plane suddenly caught fire in midair. They had been able to get back to the airport for a safe landing rather

---

[4]Jude 20. [5]Eph. 4:30. [6]1 Thes. 5:19.

than a watery Mediterranean grave as it had momentarily appeared would be their lot.

In another instance, a member of the extension committee of the Gideons International, who traveled much by air, was scheduled to depart from Montreal, Canada, on a flight to Toronto. Bad weather conditions delayed his arrival so that when he reached a connecting airport he found his flight had already left.

A ground hostess informed him and other disappointed travelers that they were to follow her to gate 41 to board another Toronto-bound plane on flight 831. Just as the Gideon representative was about to board the waiting jet the hostess called him by name and told him, "There's a seat for you on flight 277 at gate 7."

The man couldn't help feeling disgruntled at being shuttled around. Also, the plane to which he was being reassigned was, he knew, a propeller-driven one, and he preferred the smoother jet transportation. But despite his protest he was separated from his traveling companion and baggage, and directed to gate 7. The attendant there questioned his presence and made a phone call before issuing him a boarding pass. Immediately after he sat down, the plane took off.

Not until some hours later did he learn that the flight he had originally been directed to take, number 831, had crashed. The sequel and explanation became evident later. That day, five different friends had phoned his wife that the Spirit had pressured them to pray for this man because they were impressed that he was in danger. One of the five was his own minister. Obviously the Spirit does prompt prayer and one does well to heed his leadings.

Not only does the Spirit often prompt prayer but he involves himself in the prayer project. Such was the case with the prophets and teachers in the church at Antioch.[7] No doubt they were praying and fasting with a concern for spreading the gospel to countries around them. (Someone has defined fasting as the most fervent form of prayer.) In the course of their prayers the Holy Spirit conveyed to them that they were to send Paul and Barnabas forth as missionaries, which they did.

A unique, contemporary incident involves a Christian couple who were to meet a husband and wife with whom they had fellowshiped in another state where they had attended church and other meetings together. The Spirit seemed to tell the wife to take a good reference Bible to them. Her husband questioned the value or need for such a gesture, but the impression persisted.

The four had not been together long when the second wife remarked to the first, "You know, Guy has never had a Bible of his own. The one he has been carrying belongs to our granddaughter. I'm going to get him one for his birthday."

Imagine their surprise that evening when they were handed a gift-wrapped Bible and told that the Spirit had prompted the gift!

Many a call to a mission field or other vocation

---

[7]Acts 13:1-4.

has come in the course of Spirit-indited prayer.

A mother writes about prayer relative to their son's vocation. She says, "He is in college and comes home every chance he can get. A couple of months ago he came home and as usual was very happy. In his conversation he said he was changing his major in school next year. I said, 'You are?' and he said, 'Yes, I really meant to tell you and Daddy together. Two weeks ago I was at a revival. My Lord called me to be a Christian educator.' I said, 'Well, praise God; this is answered prayer.'

"I had been praying for him ever since he entered school. He was surprised about that and his father was so thrilled. About a month later his dad and I had an invitation to a town which is about an hour's drive from us, where his father was scheduled to give the main address in a meeting. In a conversation the pastor happened to mention that the church needed a youth director.

"We told him about our son and he became really interested. Later, it was a real thrill to our boy to receive a call from him, asking him to go there for an interview. He came home the following weekend to talk to his daddy about the matter. He was called to the job for the summer with all the arrangements very satisfactory. This is a blessed answer to prayer for him, his mother, and his father."

Not only is one encouraged to expect prayer reminders or inspiration to prayer through the Holy Spirit, but also one may rejoice in the fact that the Holy Spirit prays for him. "And in the same way — by our faith — the Holy Spirit helps us with our daily problems and in our praying. For we don't even know what we should pray for, nor how to pray as we should; but the Holy Spirit prays for us with such feeling that it cannot be expressed in words."[8]

There are instances where a child of God has been undergoing deep trial or has been weighed down with despair. Then, unaccountably the weight lifted. His sorrow changed to gladness and his depression to assurance. How was he to account for it? The Spirit had doubtless been interceding on his behalf. But how rarely do Christians recognize the Spirit's intercessory ministry on their behalf, and thank him for it. We miss many exciting prayer experiences through our lack of appreciation for the Holy Spirit's part in prayer.

This fact points up our need for more of the true spirit of prayer. We need to pray for it because of our inexperience in prayer, our difficulties in prayer, our faintness in prayer, our lethargy, our ignorance, our selfishness, even our very abominableness[9] in prayer.

As one confessed, "It takes time and energy to pray. To be honest, if I followed Satan I would just forget it, but I know God wants me to pray, and that's what I do daily."

Yes, God wants us to pray, not for his sake, not because he has to be coaxed for favors or

---

[8]Romans 8:26, TLB.   [9]Prov. 28:9.

persuaded to act, but because of what praying will do *in us.* And among the blessings he arranges through prayer is the excitement of seeing the thing happen that we had asked for, and of feeling that we had a part in it by our intercession.

A fifty-year-old man became dissatisfied with his vocation so he talked to his wife and to the Lord about it. He was impressed to give up his job and return to college. With his wife's co-operation, aided by her employment and home-making for his three sons, he succeeded in earning his B.A. and M.A. degrees.

By that time, however, the teaching field had become crowded and positions were hard to obtain. He received a one-year contract to teach in a nearby college while working toward his doctor's degree. But by the time he finished all his course work, job prospects were even dimmer than before. Application after application was filed, with no response. One brought the discouraging news that 124 applications for that particular position had been received in a single day! And by that date the zenith of the period for hiring was past.

One evening his wife was reminded to pray about a college in their very hometown which had the year before shown an interest in having her husband teach there. At the time, he was already obligated for the other position.

A little later, when the husband reached home, he said that he had been prompted to pray about the same place. He contacted the dean of the faculty and learned that they would be interested in interviewing him. As a result, he was hired and embarked on his chosen career without the family having to relocate or change their mode of life in any respect. Doesn't God do wonderful things?

PRAYER,
A NONEXCLUSIVE
PRIVILEGE

At the turn of the century Standard Oil and United Steel emerged as monopolies (they were called trusts) to such an extent that legislation was passed to curb their power. In a later era the Cloverleaf Dairy, a small concern in a midwestern community, was squeezed into bankruptcy by large national dairy concerns which wanted to monopolize the package milk market. By underselling at a loss to themselves in this particular area of operation (but making up the loss by higher prices in other regions where they were the sole operators) they eliminated this competitor and regained their monopoly in that location too.

Many other documented instances of monopoly of certain markets or commodities could be cited. In contrast, one thing is sure. There is no individual or organization which can contrive a monopoly on transacting business with God through prayer.

Prayer is one of the few universal privileges of mankind. There are no apartheid policies, caste systems, or minority group biases in the realm of prayer. Any unbeliever may pray for salvation with the assurance of being heard. Any believer who meets the conditions of effective prayer can expect to be heard when he prays. God has no racial prejudices nor national preferences.

God assured Cornelius, presumably an Italian,[1] that his prayers were heard, the same as were Jewish Peter's.[2] In fact, he used each to participate in the prayer answers of the other.

A Chinese rickshaw puller by the name of Zou injured his hand and arm and they became badly infected. When he presented himself for treatment at a·mission hospital he was told amputation would be necessary. The man feared he would not be able to work if this were done, and he would then starve to death. Prayer was offered by the mission church for his recovery. When the pain became almost unbearable he returned, but left again rather than have an amputation. The church continued to pray for his healing even while fearing he was jeopardizing his life. God heard their prayers, and the third time the man returned it was evident that he had been healed.

A native Brazilian pastor wanted to begin a work in a certain location but could find no suitable building to rent for worship. The Catholic priest had forbidden anyone to rent a house to the evangelicals.

The man continued to pray, but when nothing was available he decided to return home. The night before he was to leave, the believers

---

[1]Acts 10:1-4.   [2]Acts 10:9, 19.

held a group prayer meeting about the matter. After the meeting, the pastor privately talked to the Lord again, earnestly begging him for guidance.

The next morning before breakfast a visitor called to see the pastor. He lived on a farm ten miles distant and had heard of the need to rent a house for a preaching place. Evidently the Lord stirred him up to make the early morning contact in answer to the prayers of the Brazilian Christian and his followers.[3]

As Peter declared to Cornelius, "I see very clearly that the Jews are not God's only favorites! In every nation he has those who worship him and do good deeds and are acceptable to him."[4]

The *economically disadvantaged,* just as much as the person of wealth, has an audience with God. God is just as ready to answer the prayer of the one who rides a bicycle as the one who drives a Cadillac. It is not the resources of the one who presents the check, but of the one whose name appears as signer which determines whether a check will be honored. Jesus Christ is the name which is honored at the bank of heaven. He said, "If ye ask anything in my name, I will do it."[5]

A poor Chinese widow wanted very much for her son to be able to attend a mission secondary school but she had no means to finance it. Nor

---

[3]Reported in *Commissions,* March 1959. [4]Acts 10:34, 35, TLB. [5]John 14:14.

was the Academy able to offer assistance. The only thing that could be done was to commit the matter to the Lord in prayer. The missionary and the mother did so, the latter amid falling tears.

The next day, American visitors unexpectedly arrived, and as the missionary accompanied them from the railway station they asked if there was any particular need that they might meet. Immediately he was impressed to ignore other needs and tell them about the widow's burden. A meeting with her and her family was arranged and the result was God's answer to her prayer.

The *physically disabled,* unable to participate in activities normal persons engage in, suffer no such handicap in prayer. For instance, one time D. L. Moody had been invited to preach in a London pulpit. A spiritual atmosphere was lacking, everything seemed dead, and he went away mightily discouraged. But when he returned for the evening service he was conscious of an entirely different atmosphere. He preached with fervor.

When he gave the invitation, about five hundred people rose to their feet. That service was the beginning of a great revival in that church. In fact, Moody was called back from Dublin to assist in it. Behind that situation was this explanation. There had been a woman in the morning service who had an invalid sister. When she went home she told her about a Mr. Moody from Chicago who had preached and would do so again that night.

"What!" cried her sister. "Why, I have been praying for God to send him to London."

She then gave strict orders to her sister that she was not to be disturbed on any account. She retired to her room and spent the entire afternoon in prayer, and the evening as well. Held up before God by that bedridden saint, Moody had been endued by the Spirit with mighty power.

Diseases which segregate victims from other people do not bar them from praying to God. His ear is bent toward the disfigured leper as much as toward the physically fit. In a leper colony on foreign soil, meat was only a once or twice-yearly treat. One such Christian group had been given a little live pig at the beginning of summer and had carefully tended it with visions of a feast at Christmas. The very day before Christmas, the pig escaped from its pen and ran away!

There was only one recourse — the patients were called together to pray about the loss. Their leader raised his mutilated hands and begged God to undertake for them. He asked that the pig might find its way back.

Just before nightfall a squealing pig was heard. A neighboring villager had found the pig rooting in his garden. He knew whose it was so he caught it, tied its legs, put it in a wheelbarrow, and took it back to is owners. God hears even the prayers of ostracized lepers.

The *socially prominent* have no advantage over peasants or laborers when it comes to having prayers answered. In fact, because of the acute need, God may be more instant in answering the prayer of the poor than the rich.

A pastor and wife with three small children and a fourth on the way were without funds and needed milk for the babies. They had prayed and spread the situation before the Lord but the father was still greatly burdened about his dilemma. He left the house and walked out on a dock which extended over shallow, grass-filled water on the Atlantic seaboard.

He stood there meditating, his eyes not particularly focusing on anything. Then he became aware of something green and white lying on some of the weeds that stuck out of the water. Though it was out of arm's reach, he was nevertheless able to retrieve it with a long-handled net. He found it to be a dollar bill!

Neither does *age* or *maturity* accord exclusive prayer privileges. Eleven teen-age boys were staff workers at a denominational summer assembly complex. They were housed in a single-room dormitory. All were lads who professed to know the Lord.

One night as they lay in their bunks before going to sleep, one of them was smitten with contrition for the way he had reacted to a supervisor earlier in the day. He wanted to talk to the Lord about it. (Incidentally, he had broken a wrist bone two weeks before, and was supposed to keep it in the cast for four weeks longer.)

He said to the other fellows, "I feel like praying aloud. Do you mind if I do?"

No one objected, so he proceeded to do so.

In his prayer of repentance he also included a petition for the healing of his broken wrist. When he had finished, another boy spontaneously began to pray. One by one the others followed until all had prayed.

"Hey!" yelled the first boy, "My wrist has been healed." He arose, and with the assistance of the others, removed the cast. An active celebration followed.

The next morning he went to the supervisor and told her his arm had been healed. She was aghast that the cast had been removed, and mindful of the management's liability, told the lad that on account of insurance regulations he would have to go to the doctor and have his wrist X-rayed.

"But I know it has been healed," he insisted. "I walked on my hands last night."

The supervisor thought she would faint but she kept her poise and insisted that he must go have an X-ray taken. Arriving at the clinic, the youth did not report what had happened. He merely asked to have it X-rayed.

The doctor who had put on the cast was absent that day so a fellow-medic, not knowing how long the cast was supposed to have stayed on, had an X-ray taken. He checked the plates, found no evidence of a break, and reported the bone healed.

The following Sunday evening at church, with the doctor present, the boy gave his testimony of what God had done for him. After church the amazed doctor went immediately to the medical center and rechecked the X-ray plates. He scrutinized them with great care. There was no evidence of a break. The Lord had heard the prayers of the youths and had answered them.

Where there is a genuine need, for instance in respect to such basic matters as food, clothing, lodging, equipment, etc., God is honor bound to meet such needs because he has so promised. There is assurance in such a passage as, "But my God shall supply all your need according to his riches in glory by Christ Jesus."[6]

"Trust in the Lord, and do good; so shalt thou dwell in the land, and verily thou shalt be fed,"[7] is another, and countless more could be cited.

One must be careful, however, not to confuse needs with wants when claiming these promises. In today's affluent society it is easy to mistake luxuries for necessities. Though God is a God of abundance, and often gives double what is asked, he nowhere guarantees bonuses beyond needs.

In respect to giving double what is asked, this instance comes to mind: A Christian who lived in a rural location some miles from shopping centers saw that she would be out of lettuce before another trip to town. She entreated the Lord (it was springtime), "O Lord, put it on someone's heart to give us some lettuce." With that she dismissed the matter and thought no more of it.

That evening the woman who cleaned house for her telephoned to ask if she might come to work the next day instead of four days later as

---

[6]Phil. 4:19.   [7]Ps. 37:3.

had been agreed upon. When that matter had been settled, the caller then asked, "Would you like to have me bring you some lettuce when I come tomorrow? Ours needs thinning out." Once again God had answered prayer for a need.

But here is the illustration of his doubling what is asked. The next day the householder's husband went to a neighbor's to take a paper which concerned them. There he was given some garden-fresh lettuce. God truly does beyond what one can think or imagine![8]

A newly born-again woman, in very tight financial circumstances, wanted to attend a covered-dish dinner at the church one night. She realized that she would not have opportunity to get anything, nor would she have any money to buy it if she did. She prayed about it. Later that day she was called to do housework for a fellow-Christian without a definite understanding about remuneration. When the employer suddenly decided to go to town, she asked her helper if there was anything she wanted her to get for her.

"Yes," the woman decided. "You can get me a chicken, and take what it costs out of what you plan to pay me."

When her work was done, her employer handed her the chicken she had been asked to buy, plus the amount of money she had paid for a previous day's work, without any deductions. The

---

[8] Eph. 3:20.

worker rejoiced at how the Lord had taken care of the situation for her.

Stressing that God answers the prayers of the poor does not mean that being poor, or even bankrupt, does in itself qualify one for answered prayer. As someone has pointed out, some of the poorest people may be the stingiest, a quality that hinders effective prayer whether one is a pauper or plutocrat. What masquerades as thrift may often be pure miserliness, and thus an obstacle to answered prayer. "He who shuts his ears to the cries of the poor will be ignored in his own time of need."[9]

If one is experiencing unanswered prayer, he may do well to examine his life for selfishness. Sometimes one cannot afford to save his money. There is the warning: "It is possible to hold on too tightly and lose everything"[10] — lose prayer power as well as material substance.

Official position or *political status* convey no advantage in prayer. Daniel, Peter, and Paul suffered the humiliation of imprisonment, yet each had power in prayer.[11] The scorned publican of Bible times had prayer answered whereas the prestigious Pharisee had it denied. The accounts of these experiences make it plain that it is inward rather than outward conditions which constitute the essential factor in effective prayer.[12] We may fool ourselves or others in respect to the genuineness of our prayers, but we never fool

[9]Pr. 21:13, TLB.   [10]Pr. 11:24, TLB.   [11]Dan. 9:3-22; Acts 9:40, 41; 10:9; Eph. 3:1.   [12]Lu. 18:10-14.

God. He knows the degree of our earnestness. There was obvious sincerity in the publican's prayer in contrast to the Pharisee's hypocritical superficiality.

Queen Victoria of England, known for her piety, doubtless had prayers answered, but so did some of her humblest, poorest subjects. George Washington, President of the United States, is often pictured in the posture of prayer, but an unknown and unnoted drummer boy may have been equally powerful in prayer. It is not *who* prays, but *how* one prays that matters.

Note the *alls* in this passage, "The Lord is nigh unto all them that call upon him, to all that call upon him in truth."[13]

Therefore, because prayer is a non-exclusive privilege, any one who prays in accord with biblical principles may find himself involved in thrilling experiences.

---

[13]Ps. 145:18.

PRAYER
CIRCLES THE
GLOBE

Coca Cola or other commercial interests may claim their products are to be found everywhere on the earth, but actually there is no other item so universally available to mankind as prayer. From the bottom of the sea to the moon itself prayer can be offered. Jonah prayed from the belly of a fish.[1] At the equator or the Arctic, prayer may be voiced to God. From the humid jungles of the Amazon or the barren wastes of Siberia, prayer may ascend to God. There is no location, situation, or nation where prayer cannot be breathed.

Near Danang in Vietnam is a home for children. One day a boy was bitten on his big toe by a bamboo viper. Antivenom was immediately injected but he needed hospital treatment, and there was no boat available. Prayer was offered about the emergency. In just a few minutes a helicopter passed over, and they succeeded in waving it down. Later, the pilot explained, "I just felt I had to fly over the beach and take a look. There was the doctor waving me down."[2]

---

[1]Jonah 2:1.   [2]Reported in *World Vision Heartline*, June 1971.

Even legislation cannot throttle the spirit of prayer though it may prevent its articulation. Neither is there any person, condition, or matter which may not be a subject of prayer, because God created and controls the universe. Therefore nothing can be beyond the scope of prayer. Everything, everywhere, is eligible to be prayed about.

For instance, one of mankind's continuous concerns is the weather, and it is an acceptable subject for prayer. The Bible supports the fact in such passages as these:

"When the skies are shut and there is no rain because of our sins, and then we pray toward this Temple and claim you as our God, and turn from our sins because you have punished us, then listen from heaven and forgive the sins of your people, and teach them what is right; and send rain upon this land which you have given to your people as their own property."[3]

"If I shut up the heavens so that there is no rain, or if I command the locust swarms to eat up all of your crops, or if I send an epidemic among you, then if my people will humble themselves and pray, and search for me, and turn from their wicked ways, I will hear them from heaven and forgive their sins and heal their land."[4]

Elijah prayed for a withholding of rain and then a release of rain and both prayers were honored. Contemporary folk have had similar

---

[3] 2 Chr. 6:26, 27, TLB.   [4] 2 Chr. 7:13, 14, TLB.

experience. The little Arab community of Chad had no rain and feared a drouth was in prospect. This was a serious matter for a people dependent on crops for food. Simon Baigoto gave this report of the circumstances:[5]

Pagan religious leaders had been given gifts to pray for rain but this had brought no results. There was consequent discouragement for all. All, that is, except three Christians who united in prayer and fasting that the situation might be usable to God in opening the area to the gospel.

First, they asked God to withhold rain for three more days. During that time they announced that there would be public prayer for rain on the following Sunday. Having assurance from the Spirit that God was going to honor their faith, they invited the Government Administrator, the Secretary and his helpers, the local chief and his men, and others to attend. At 10:30 on the designated morning, a motley group assembled under a cloudless sky.

The leader explained the purpose of the meeting and told the people, "We have invited you today to see what God will do so that you will know that the true way to God is through the Lord Jesus Christ."

As he was reading the story of Elijah from 1 Kings 18:25-46, thunder began to roll. Soon the rain was falling in torrents, and it didn't stop raining for three days!

---

[5]Reported in *Horizons*, Jan./Feb. 1970.

"Ask the Lord for rain in the springtime, and he will answer with lightning and showers. Every field will become a lush pasture."[6]

Another instance of prayer about weather conditions is one where a Christian long experienced in prayer had working for her a neighbor of limited means. One day the neighbor expressed a wish that the frost would hold off until their beans had matured and been harvested.

Knowing that a good bean crop would help much in providing their food for the coming winter, the employer asked, "How much longer do you need for the beans to grow?"

"Two or three weeks," was the reply, "we were late in getting them planted."

The praying woman looked at the calendar. It was the first week in October and killing frosts might come any time in that locality. They had been known to occur even in September.

"I know you need your beans," she commented. "You keep looking after them as they require. I'm going to ask the Lord to delay a freeze until after they have matured."

In the days ahead there were several cold nights, and the weather bureau warned of the danger of frost on each occasion. The intercessor continued to remind the Lord of her request. The frost failed to come each time. In fact, although some snow fell, the needy couple were able to harvest a fine bean crop.

"I never before picked beans out from under

---

[6]Zech. 10:1, TLB.

the snow," the husband of the working woman told her employer.

"Didn't your wife tell you that we had asked the Lord to give you a bean crop?" she asked.

"Yes," he answered, "but we didn't have faith to count on it."

They had all the beans they could use and can, and sold over twenty bushels as well as giving away some. The first killing frost occurred on the night of October 31st.

Health is certainly a universal need, and one that can be prayed about by anyone anywhere. Proof of this is found in the case of a Christian wife whose eyes became infected. It seemed perhaps to have been an allergic reaction to the pollen of some weeds she had pulled. Her ailment was diagnosed by a specialist as iritis. Treatment was ineffectual, and she was practically without eyesight. Blindness seemed in prospect, with no assurance that medical treatment could prevent it. Prayer was offered by her family, pastor, and fellow Christians as well as by friends far away.

The couple had provided equipment for a mission station in Africa, and when word of the difficulty reached there, the situation was placed before the native Christians for prayer. The problem gripped one young native pastor in particular and he became burdened and prayed intensely about it. So heavily did the matter weigh on his heart that he told the Lord, "My eyes for hers, only let her see and I shall be willing to lose my sight." And according to the report, he actually did suffer loss of it for a time. The sequel was that the American woman did recover her sight, and according to their calculations her improvement dated from the day the man so earnestly interceded for her. The woman is convinced that the restoration of her sight was definitely in answer to prayer.

Many Christian organizations issue prayer calendars citing particular persons to be prayed for on specific dates (often for missionaries on their birthdays). Countless testimonies have been recorded, of perils avoided, obstacles removed, or problems resolved in correlation with such dates — all of which verifies the fact of prayer's globe-circling influence.

The explanation for all of this is, of course, an omnipresent, omniscient, and omnipotent God. Because he is everywhere, knows all things, and can do all things, prayer can be offered anywhere and be effective anywhere. To be affiliated with God in such prayer means that a common, ordinary person shares an experience with the greatest Person in the universe, one who has a more complete knowledge and intense concern than anyone else anywhere.

The Scriptures afford these reminders about God:

"The eyes of Jehovah are in every place, beholding the evil and the good."[7] "For God is closely watching you, and he weighs carefully everything you do."[8] "Thine, O Lord, is the

---

[7] Pr. 15:3.   [8] Pr. 5:21, TLB; cf. 2 Chr. 16:9a; Job 34:21a.

greatness, and the power, and the glory, and the victory, and the majesty: for all that is in the heaven and in the earth is thine; thine is the kingdom, O Lord, and thou art exalted as head above all.

"Riches and honor come from you alone, and you are the Ruler of all mankind; your hand controls power and might, and it is at your discretion that men are made great and given strength."[9]

In view of these facts, why shouldn't people anywhere pray about everything? God commands it: ". . . in *everything* by prayer and supplication with thanksgiving let your requests be made known unto God."[10]

It is important to note here that gratitude is a required element in prayer. Too often that is overlooked. We make requests, but much less often we express thanks for favors already given, or yet to be received. Yet the Scripture says, "No matter what happens, always be thankful, for this is God's will for you who belong to Christ Jesus."[11]

A child of God whose husband has cancer, consistently rejoices in the Lord. Letters to friends carry statements like these: "We feel God has been so good to us." "My post office work has been such a blessing to us." "We are being so blessed." Obviously she has appropriated God's

[9]1 Chr. 29:12, TLB.   [10]Phil. 4:6, cf. also 1 Tim. 2:8.
[11]1 Th. 5:18, TLB.

grace to "rejoice evermore."[12] She not only requests, she thanks, too.

Even in the matter of death, prayer can be effective. A missionary in South America reports that their language teacher, a Christian national, was called to accompany her devout but unsaved mother to the hospital. Deeply concerned for her parent's salvation, she tenderly nursed her in her terminal illness. Just three days before her death, the mother received Christ as her Savior.

An agonizing death had been the doctor's prediction for the woman. Naturally she dreaded it. The daughter, knowing this, had been asking God to spare her mother such an experience. He heard. The woman went to be with the Lord at dawn one morning as she slept. The peaceful expression on her face was evidence to the daughter at her side that God had answered her prayer.

In view of the unlimited scope and influence of prayer, one must recognize it as an opportunity to engage in projects with the greatest possibilities this side of eternity, and with no limit to what may be undertaken or accomplished. Moreover, there is always the element of excitement because one never knows in what manner or under what circumstances a prayer will be answered.

A young woman had long had a burden to witness to a certain neighbor. She had made it a matter of prayer, and kept watching for a chance to do so. She would walk past the woman's

---

[12]1 Th. 5:16.

house, even knock at her door, but she got no response and never found an opportunity to talk to her. At last she became rather rebellious about the matter since she was so anxious to witness to the woman but was frustrated in trying to do so.

One day she was very busy at home. She had her washer running and was ironing at the same time. The telephone rang. She unplugged the iron and took down the receiver to find it was her husband calling her. He had to leave his office on business and wanted her to come stay there in his absence. She was very reluctant to do so because she felt she had too much to do at home.

"Can't you just shut the office during the lunch hour?" she asked, since it was near noon. He said he was expecting a telephone call, and did not want to leave without someone to answer the phone. Very unwillingly she closed the house and drove to his office.

Only a few minutes after her husband had gone, in walked the very lady she had been praying to see! She had her opportunity to testify, no one came in, the phone did not ring, and there were no distractions. Her prayer for a chance to witness was answered though not at the time or place she might have chosen. She had very nearly refused to rearrange her plans so God could work everything together for good.

This points up the fact that God does not always answer prayer in the manner we expect. A Christian married woman, not yet in the senior age bracket, lost her hearing and was forced to use a hearing aid which was far from satisfactory. She had prayed much about it, and often had visualized the Lord healing her miraculously as he had the deaf during his days on earth. Instead, the Lord brought to her attention a new type of surgery by which her hearing might be restored. The operation was successful, and she praised God for answered prayer, though it had not come about in the manner she had imagined. Nor do we always recognize, at least at first, that God knows better than we do, what is best for us.

A woman who had been asked to fill in temporarily in a government office as an accommodation to a friend, had opportunity to take an examination for a permanent place. She asked the Lord for guidance because she was uncertain what to do about it.

One morning she awoke with a feeling of pressure and urgency to apply for the examination. Later she learned that that day was the last one on which she could have filed an application.

She took the examination and passed it. But instead of being assigned to the office where she had been working, as she had assumed she would be, she was placed in another, though not very distant, office.

The prospect of change made her very unhappy. She had been close friends with her supervisor, and because the two lived in the same locality, they could ride to and from work together. She prayed about it, and asked others to pray that she could adjust to the situation.

It developed in a short time that it had been a case of "disappointments: his appointments," because the supervisor was relocated in the same office. Neither one of the women had had any idea she would be. It was proof of the Scripture, ". . . we know not what to pray for as we ought,"[13] that is, we are not always aware of what to pray for, but we can rejoice that the Spirit makes intercession for us according to the will of God, who "always gives his best to those who leave the choice to him."

---

[13]Rom. 8:26.

PERSONAL —
PERTINENT —
PRACTICAL

A Christian couple met a person interested in buying a parcel of land they owned, so they concluded the Lord meant for them to dispose of it. Following a series of contacts (accompanied by private prayer for guidance on the part of the couple) it seemed that agreement had been reached on details of the deal. A date and hour was set for closing of the transaction.

The morning it was to occur, the couple prayed, "Lord, if this is not your will, or not the best thing for both parties involved, just don't let Mr. R. get here."

About half an hour before he was to have arrived, the telephone rang and he excused himself because of the unexpected arrival of guests. The couple were awestruck by this turn of affairs. Moreover, as the days passed, the man never did contact them. In the course of a few weeks, however, they were approached by another buyer, a stranger, who offered them a better price and terms. A sale was made, one more advantageous than the other would have been. How exciting it was to see the hand of God in these events!

When you have a desire or need for something,

be it commodity or service, tangible or intangible, you make contact with a person or firm you presume could give you satisfaction. What follows is termed "doing business" with them. *Prayer is doing business with God,* and is every bit as practical as any earthly transaction.

The foregoing true story does not mean one uses God. Rather, one meets the conditions which allow him to co-work with human beings. Moreover, prayer is not conveying wishes to a divine Santa Claus, nor is it like telephoning an order to the druggist, or filling out a requisition slip.

The inspired Rule Book makes clear the conditions of effectual prayer: a right motive, a petition that is for the best interests for all concerned, and a willingness to accept yes, no, or wait awhile for an answer.

One had as well keep his mouth shut unless he prays believing that God *can* and *will* (under the above conditions) answer him. The Bible says, "You can never please God without faith, without depending on him. Anyone who wants to come to God must believe that there is a God and that he rewards those who sincerely look for him."[1]

An example of a wrong motive might be the case of a woman praying that her husband would be cured of drinking to excess. What actually prompted her prayer was the deprivation, embarrassment, and loss of social status that his alcoholism brought on his family. Her request

---

[1] Hebrews 11:6, **TLB**.

was not prompted by concern for the man's welfare or future, nor the alteration of the distorted image this man presented of the God who created him.

On the other hand, an unselfish motive can prompt a God-approved prayer which he would delight to answer. For example, it may be remembered that on one occasion four United States airmen were kidnapped and held by Turkish leftists, then later released. Here is the prayer background for their deliverance:

J. W. Brooks, a deacon in the Galatian Baptist Mission of Ankara, Turkey, was a commander of the detachment from which they were kidnapped. He testified that he had prayed for their safe return from the very beginning, but on the fifth morning he felt impressed to pray specifically that they would be released that very day.

It was in the evening of that day that a police car drove up to the apartment building in which the four were held captive. The policeman had come in answer to a routine call in an upstairs apartment and knew nothing of the airmen being held in the same building.

The kidnappers, seeing the official car, prepared to shoot it out, thinking the police had discovered their hideout. After a short while the policeman left the building and drove away. The kidnappers thought that he was going for reinforcements. Up to this point they had not planned to set the airmen free. Thinking they had been discovered, the kidnappers slipped out of the windows of the apartment, leaving the Americans in their tiny room. After a period of silence, the airmen cautiously left their room, then the apartment, and when it seemed safe, the building. They then hailed a taxi, which returned them to their quarters.[2]

Deacon Brooks testified that he felt that these events did not just happen but were evidence that God had intervened in answer to prayer. A more publicized kidnapping was the case of Barbara Jane Mackle, college student, and daughter of wealthy parents. She was held for ransom and all the law forces of the country were alerted to render assistance in saving her life and apprehending the kidnappers.

Probably few people are aware that prayer was a decisive factor in her deliverance. The director of the FBI affirms that it was. Asked to cite an instance where prayer was answered in a way that was helpful, he cited this case and said, "Along with my associates, I knew we would need help beyond ourselves to find the young girl."

It will be remembered that she was finally found encased in a coffin-like box and buried in an isolated woodland of scrub bushes, trees, and vines. That only God could have led the searchers to discover her is attested by the director's statement, "We in the FBI believe that our prayers made the difference that day."[3]

Prayer may be the normal routine for daily

---

[2]Reported by Foreign Mission Board, S.B.C., April 1971. [3]Reported in *Decision*, July, 1971.

operations on either a personal or group level. For example, as a result of prayer, what began as a tiny mission church in Nebraska, housed in a small, dilapidated building with only four families active in its ministry, became a thriving church occupying a fine building. The achievement was one of suspense and drama, but a valid illustration that prayer is practical.

The membership realized that for many reasons a new building was a necessity. They began talking to the Lord about it. Someone suggested a desirable site about half a mile away, and it was voted to contact the owner.

This turned out to be a Catholic lady in her eighties and she was very vehement in her refusal to sell. After several fruitless interviews with her, and based upon conviction born in prayer, it was decided to contact the woman once more and offer her $12,000 for the piece of land.

Before she could be contacted, however, she herself telephoned and explained that something had come into her life to make her decide to sell, and that she would do so for $12,000! Thirty days after the date of sale, the woman died. Her heirs would never have sold the land at that price.

Now the little mission was confronted with the need of money for construction. Again they prayed unitedly. The denominational mission board had loaned money to help purchase the land but would help no more until it was paid for. The banks were not minded to make a loan. So the building effort seemed stalled, but the group kept praying earnestly.

About this time they heard of a Texan who was helping churches build as a service to the Lord. He could draw plans. He was contacted and in less than a fortnight he drove up to counsel with them.

Through personal sacrifices the loan for the land had been paid off so a set of plans were submitted to the denominational board. They were rejected because they called for a basement. A second plan was drawn and submitted. It was accepted, but because of the small membership, not enough signers were available for the loan application. The Texas man returned to his home and came back in three days with the required number of signatures, all in answer to prayer! The mission board granted a $23,000 loan.

In the meantime, the membership had heard of a group in Louisiana who took their vacation time to help build churches. They were called long distance but the response was that they were booked up for that year. To the mission membership this was just a challenge to more earnest prayer.

There was a man in the Nebraska community who was experimenting with modular housing. He was called in and agreed to furnish a complete understructure at cost because it would be the first in the state, and would constitute a sort of demonstration project. But first there would have to be a foundation.

More trouble had been encountered when application was made for a building permit. It was claimed that there was a high water table and no sewer system in that area, therefore the application was tabled. Usually such an action was tantamount to refusal, but not to this little knot of believers. They believed all things were possible with God so they went to him about the matter at the Wednesday night prayer meeting. Unexplainably, at a called meeting of the city council the request was taken from the table and the building permit granted, an action without precedent.

Another unexpected development was a call from the Louisiana group reporting that one of their dates had been postponed, and therefore they could arrive and begin work the following Monday. Rejoicing over this was short lived because Satan was busy, as usual, and trolled the man who was to do the footings off on a fishing trip, postponing his availability.

More prayer was offered, and one of the members was impressed to call his brother, a worker in construction trades in Kansas City, to see if he could suggest a way out of the dilemma. Men who might respond in the emergency were a hundred miles away for a weekend of fishing, but they were contacted and agreed to return and travel to Nebraska to pour the 3200 square feet of concrete. They were to drive all night and arrive by eleven, Saturday morning.

The company which was supplying the concrete had to be notified by that hour to start the trucks of concrete rolling toward the construction site or they would not do so until the following Monday. At 10:55 A.M., with the Kansas City crew not yet there, a prayer meeting was held. It was decided that with faith in God, the concrete haulers would be given the green light to come ahead.

Another complication was that an arrangement had been made with a nearby fire station to permit use of a fire hydrant for water. They had not only given permission, but had even laid hose to enable it. At that juncture, the city manager interfered and decreed that the city would not furnish one drop of water. Other arrangements had to be made, but as a result of prayer, water for the project was hauled in from another source.

At 11:10 A.M. the Kansas City crew arrived and were ready to start pouring concrete when the first batch arrived. Another threat to success, also coped with by prayer, was a huge black rain cloud which hovered at the edge of the city all day. Not until 9 o'clock that night did it begin to release its moisture.

So the concrete was poured, ready for the Louisiana group to begin building on Monday morning after their Sunday arrival. It was like Nehemiah's "So built we the wall . . . for the people had a mind to work" and, in this case, to *pray*. The membership truly believes that their church building is a monument to answered prayer.

Prayer is often multifactored, even though the one who offers the petition may not be aware that it is. Seldom does one make a request of God which does not involve the affairs of other people — persons, perhaps, whom the one who prays does not even know exist.

For example, a commercial gardener prays for a bumper crop which he will be able to market at a nice profit. It might be that if a very large quantity of that particular product were thrown on the market all at one time, it would glut the market and result in loss to other growers. Perhaps a surplus of that commodity would lessen the demand for another item, and this would work a hardship on someone else. It might even affect import and export quotations, balance of trade operations, or what not. Our finite minds cannot encompass all the ramifications of a single situation, but God can, and he must act accordingly, justly, and impartially for the benefit of all. Therefore we must be willing for him to refuse our requests on occasion, knowing that ". . . all things work together for good to them that love God. . . ."[4] In order for all circumstances to mesh, God may have to delay the answer to one's prayers.

A church was without a pastor and was seeking one. Their pulpit committee was impressed that they should secure a certain man, and prayed that they might, but when he was contacted he decisively said no. Another man was ultimately called. He served for a period during which he was used of God to correct some bad situations, but neither the pastor nor the membership were

---

[4]Romans 8:28.

happy in their relationship, so he eventually resigned.

Once again the church's pulpit committee waited on the Lord for guidance. Again they felt directed to the man they had previously contacted but who had rejected their overture. He was again approached, and this time he responded.

"There were conditions in your church under which I could not have worked," he explained, "but I understand they have been remedied, therefore I will come."

God had to make that church wait awhile until the time and situation were ripe for answering prayer.

A Christian car dealer bought a new wrecker truck and was anxious to sell his old one. When he saw his salesman dealing with a person who he thought might be a prospect he called him aside and reminded him about it, quoting a price that would be acceptable. Then he prayed the Lord to give them a sale for it. But the prospect did not buy it. Later, another man came in and offered fifty dollars more for it and was glad to get it.

In a period when the housing situation in a metropolitan district was critically tight, a couple were told the duplex they rented had been sold and that they would have to move. Aghast at the difficulties they foresaw, they immediately went to the Lord, asking him to undertake for them. They spread the word of their dilemma to others, and asked them for prayer support.

So acute was the rental shortage that very

few ads appeared in the classified section of the daily paper. Moreover, information they contained on vacancies was often "leaked" to friends by the paper's staff before the advertisement reached the readers. Nevertheless, the couple faithfully checked the columns daily for any lead they might offer. Their situation seemed almost desperate as the day they must vacate their apartment approached.

On a Sunday morning, having made ready to depart for Sunday school and church, the wife sat down to peruse the rental ads. There was absolutely nothing offered that could serve their purposes. For various reasons they did not feel that buying property was in the Lord's program for them at that time.

For that reason the wife could not account for her eyes straying down to the "For Sale" column which followed the "For Rent" one, but she read the first listing and then reread it.

"Listen," she told her husband, "this for sale ad says gas, water, and electricity furnished. That sounds like a place for rent rather than for sale." They investigated at once, verified that the ad had been placed in the wrong category, and found the duplex apartment exactly suited to their needs in every respect. They never doubted that God was responsible for the erroneous listing which worked on their behalf.

On another occasion they had spent six weeks on a southern island and wanted to remain longer but their reservation had run out and other tenants were scheduled to move in. Here too, because of the annual influx of winter visitors, the housing situation was tight. They made various contacts at motels and realtors, but could find nothing suited to their needs.

Meanwhile, they had made it a matter of prayer, asking the Lord if he wanted them to remain on the island, to open up a place for them. One day the wife went for a walk and was astonished to see a *For Rent* sign on a private cottage.

When she made inquiry, she learned that it had been reserved for a customary New York renter but illness had forced a cancellation. For some reason the owners had not yet advertised or listed the vacancy with the Chamber of Commerce or realtors. Assured that the Lord had definitely arranged it for them, the couple moved in, not only for the balance of that season, but for several to follow.

Just as all business deals are not sizable nor sensational, so all prayer transactions may not be significant except on a personal level. For example, a Christian couple had enjoyed a vacation in a resort area. In the course of their return home they paused in a metropolitan area to shop and attend a meeting. Rain began to fall, requiring them to don rain gear. Later, as they continued the trip home, after they had left the city behind, the wife discovered she had lost an earring.

She did not know when or where she had lost it, but speculated that she had brushed it off when she put on a rain bonnet as she got out of the car in a parking lot. The earring consisted of a nugget-type, semiprecious stone which her husband had bought for her in a distant state. She was unhappy about the loss, and besought the Lord about it several times in the days that followed.

About a week later she drove to her county seat to do some shopping. Expecting to put a box of groceries in the trunk, she took her key and unlocked it. As the lid opened, there before her lay the lost earring. To her it was a miraculous answer to prayer because they had no recollection of her helping pack luggage in the car preparatory to starting home, or en route, nor had the husband seen the earring when he unpacked the car.

Another child of God gave this testimony about prayer in daily life. She had put a ten-dollar bill in a letter to her son. This was unwise, of course. A check or money order would have been more prudent, and in accord with the Scripture, "Thou shalt not make trial of the Lord thy God." No sooner had she mailed it than she realized she had forgotten to seal the letter. A call to the post office brought the information that the mail had already gone out.

She took her anxiety and need to the Lord and asked him to take care of the situation. In due time the son did receive the letter with the currency enclosed. She testified regarding this and other answers to prayer: "I give God the glory when I ask and he answers."

There are, of course, hindrances to praying effectively. More will be said of that later, but right here let it be stressed that the Bible indicates that disobedience or sin of any kind prevents God from blessing us with the answer we would like to have. "If I regard iniquity in my heart, the Lord will not hear me."[5]

The Scripture specifically mentions stinginess, marital disharmony, unforgiveness, selfishness, and doubt as obstacles to answered prayer.[6] One must sincerely observe all the conditions of effective prayer if he is to experience successful transactions with God.

---

[5]Ps. 66:18.　[6]See Pr. 21:13; 1 Pet. 3:8; Mk. 11:25; Jas. 4:3; Heb. 11:6.

NO HARMFUL
SIDE EFFECTS

An important factor for consideration of medical measures to treat the world's diseases is the question of damaging side effects. There are medications which can be used for particular ailments and which will unquestionably counteract certain undesirable conditions. But at the same time they also initiate other undesirable reactions.

Happily, the use of prayer has no adverse accompaniments. Its side effects are all on the plus side. Along with achieving its primary goal, the answer to the prayer, it may simultaneously bestow other blessings. In fact, one suspects that this may have been one of God's primary purposes in arranging the prayer partnership with man. How important, then, that we give them due consideration.

Prayer fosters unselfishness. This is a particularly helpful aspect of prayer with others. As we participate in group prayer we become aware of the longings, problems, and needs of fellowmen. We share their interests and become concerned for their prayers to be answered. This often prompts additional prayer in private for their objects.

Sometimes it helps us get a better perspective on our attitudes and wants. We recognize that our prayers have been "I" centered instead of "other" oriented. Often it helps us to realize we need only shoes, whereas the other fellow needs feet!

Prayer develops patience. It is a testing ground for perseverence. Too often we are like children shopping with their mothers and wanting everything they see. One Christian declares, "I'm thankful the Lord knows better than to answer all the fool prayers I've prayed."

Prayer promotes maturity. When a child of God came across a prayer list she had used a decade ago, she was embarrassed by the immaturity of some of her desires. Maturity consists somewhat in being able to take all factors into consideration and to take a long-range view of possible outcomes. As one ponders the elements involved in praying effectively, and the conditions which may constitute barriers to it, he grows spiritually. He becomes more able to be objective, more tolerant of disappointments, less biased and impulsive. Given a period of growth, Peter would not have begged, "Lord, not my feet only, but also my hands and my head."

Prayer encourages serenity. The fact that the answer to our prayers does not depend on us, that it is a free gift from the Lord,[1] for which we

---

[1] Rom. 8:32.

need neither work nor strive to deserve, should dissipate much of our tension. To know that we are doing business with the greatest power in the universe, and co-working with its most merciful and gracious Personality, should dispel all worry.

A man active in the Lord's work had a stroke when a blood clot lodged in an artery, shutting off blood to his brain. Surgery was a calculated risk but necessary to save his life. Christian friends rallied to the couple and upheld them in prayer. The wife testified, "Two hours before Oscar came out of surgery, God lifted the burden and anxiety."[2]

One person has defined prayer as a time exposure of the soul to God. "It is quiet meditation, a wordless communion, a patient waiting for a new revelation."[3]

Such a concept and practice of prayer will endue one with composure and gentleness.

Prayer channels power. Long ago prayer was defined as the breath of the soul. The aptness of that definition is shown by a recent invention. An electrical switch has been devised which is activated by human breath. A totally disabled person, by the mere adjustment of his breath, can tune a television set, type up to one hundred words a minute, and perform other chores. The power of breathing in such an operation parallels remarkably the power of prayer. Both make possible results which could not otherwise be attained.

---

[2]*War Cry,* June 17, 1971. [3]Mildred Long, *Adult Class,* 1950 Judson Press.

Prayer gladdens the heart. Prayer is spending time with God. How can one commune with the most wonderful of all beings without being thrilled by it? One rejoices at what has already come to pass in his life and the resources that are his through prayer. He is made glad by the fellowship with God, by the release from stress, by the prospect of the outcome.

Prayers of praise especially do this for one. Many are the testimonies that when one who was feeling discouraged began to thank God for his blessings, and praise him for his goodness, it resulted in the depression being lifted. It is a good practice to begin every prayer with thanksgiving and praise. (The former rejoices in the gift, the latter in the Giver.) Then after that, one can make petitions and intercede.

The habit of praise expands one's personality and improves his health. Doctors have even been known to prescribe thanksgiving as a daily therapy which produces results. "With Jesus' help we will continually offer our sacrifice of praise to God by telling others of the glory of his name."[4]

Prayer imparts radiance. When Moses came from the presence of God his face was so aglow that people could not look upon him. He had to wear a veil when he mingled with them. The person who communes often and intimately with the Lord can become so filled with the Spirit that his face too will glow. That must have been why people beholding Peter and John "took

---

[4]Heb. 13:15, TLB.

knowledge of them that they had been with Jesus."[5]

Obviously prayer is a many-faceted jewel, a wonderful and glorious privilege, yet at the same time a serious responsibility. One need not, however, carry this responsibility alone. He has the Holy Spirit interceding as he prays[6] and also Christ, sitting at the right hand of God.[7] It is he and we coordinating in entreaty to God that results in our petitions being granted.

Thus it is that when we engage in prayer along these lines, God's purposes are served and the one who prays is enhanced. Scripturally pursued, prayer changes the life of the one who prays, puts a thrill in his heart as he sees God work, and imparts a radiance to his face as he comes from the prayer closet.

Mary Slessor, the fervent missionary to Africa, wrote, "My life is one long, daily, hourly record of answered prayer. For physical health, for mental overstrain, for guidance given marvelously, for errors and dangers averted, for enmity to the gospel subdued, for food provided at the exact hour needed, for everything that goes to make up life and my poor service, I can testify, with a full and often wonder-stricken awe, that I know God answers prayer."[8]

Undoubtedly she would have testified, if asked, that prayer is exciting!

---

[5]Acts 4:13.   [6]Rom. 8:26.   [7]Heb. 7:25.   [8]*Herald of His Coming*, Oct. 1971.

POWER
FAILURE

By now you may have realized you're wired for prayer but the power has never been turned on. Perhaps so-called prayer has been just by rote or a ritual of yours, an emergency exercise, or a rabbit's-foot deal.

Although God has known this all along, he would not commandeer your lines or appropriate your facilities except by your request. That is one aspect of prayer not often mentioned. Prayer is God's safeguard against trespassing on man's free will. He awaits your desire and "application for power" before extending his service over your equipment.

Besides that element, there is the condition of your equipment. Maybe it is not safe for high voltage transmission. There may be power leaks (bad habits), short circuits (sin), or worn insulation (worldliness), that would result in shocks, explosions, or burn-outs. In fact your whole system may need replacement before you could become a safe transformer or cable. How can that come about?

First, you yourself must recognize and admit to God what rickety, shoddy material you are.[1] Then you must ask him to reconstitute you[2] into a usable, reliable conduction system capable of efficient transmission. (It must be kept constantly in mind that we humans are never a *source* of power, only a *channel* for the transmission of divine power by means of prayer.)

There is also the possibility that your prayer lines are in order, that you have even had prayer communication, but now you have prayer failure. Your prayers are not being answered. As mentioned previously, the cause of this is very probably sin in your Christian life.

All of us have had experience with our electricity being off. It creates various kinds of crises, from a life and death matter in a hospital to one on a personal level such as having to brush your teeth by hand!

The dismaying thing about it may be that it is not necessarily a bomb drop or some big catastrophe that causes it. For instance, a power failure was once caused by a tiny bullet nick in the insulation of one of the power lines. Or we've read of a woodpecker or a squirrel disrupting service. That is the way it is with our spiritual lives. It is the seemingly trivial things that often render us powerless and hinders prayer.

We are all aware that we have a Power Source in God through Christ.[3] We know there

---

[1]Rom. 3:23; Isa. 64:6; Tit. 3:5. [2]Jn. 3:7; 2 Cor. 5:17; Rom. 12:1, 2. [3]Acts 1:8.

will never be a power failure at the Source. Jesus gave that assurance.[4]

Power failure is possible due to short circuits in the power channels of *praying* and *abiding*. That these two items do constitute our power channels is attested by Scripture: "And we are sure of this, that he will listen to us whenever we ask him for anything in line with his will. And if we really know he is listening when we talk to him and make our requests, then we can be sure that he will answer us."[5] "But if you stay in me and obey my commands, you may ask any request you like, and it will be granted."[6]

What "little things" can cause power failure in the life of a Christian? Obviously they may fall in any of these categories: thoughts, looks, words, acts.

Would you want all the thoughts you had last Sunday in church framed and hung as pictures? Why not? What did God think of your thoughts?

A few years ago Trans World Airlines at Fairfax Airport in Kansas City constructed what was supposed to be an electrically perfect room, size 8 x 10 feet, in which mechanics were to work entirely sealed off from all electrical distractions. Very special construction techniques were employed to make it so. But when it was complete and an ohmmeter reading was taken, it was found there was a small amount of conduction somewhere. After hours of searching, testing, and measuring with all kinds of detectors and gauges, it was discovered that the trouble lay in lead pen-

---

[4]Matt. 28:18.   [5]1 Jn. 5:14, 15, TLB.   [6]Jn. 15:7, TLB.

cil marks on the lumber placed there by the carpenters when they measured the two by fours for sawing. The graphite in the pencil mark was the cause of their trouble.

A suspicious thought, a critical one, an irritable one, a condemning one, to say nothing of doubt, discouragement, or rebellion, may be the pencil mark that interferes with our contact with God.

Then there may be power failures due to facial expressions (which, of course, reflect our thoughts). Did you ever have the experience of being robbed of your poise by a glance? Your eyes met your mate's and you thought, *what did I say or do wrong?* Or another person's eyes swept over you and you wondered, *has my wig slipped over one ear?*

We are told that a shred of lint from clothing or moisture from a finger print can make a guided missile zooming along at twice the speed of sound miss its mark. Insignificant as a look may seem, if it makes another person uncomfortable or unhappy, it may be the cause of power failure in our prayer life.

"An high look is sin . . ."[7] ". . . whosoever looketh on a woman to lust after her hath committed adultery with her already in his heart . . ."[8] "Look not thou upon the wine when it is red, when it giveth his color in the cup, when it moveth itself aright."[9] Whenever we have a power failure we had better think about our eyes and the possible sin of which they may have been guilty.

---

[7]Pr. 21:4.   [8]Matt. 5:28.   [9]Pr. 23:31.

The wayward words we speak are the product of our thoughts: "For as he thinketh in his heart, so is he . . ."[10] We need not be reminded of what a crisis an ill-advised word can create. It happens often in our churches and other organizations. It is like one time in New York when someone tossed an empty beverage can in front of a subway train just as it was entering a tunnel under the East River. The result was an hour-and-a-half tie-up that affected fifty-five trains and seventy-five thousand passengers at the height of the evening rush period.

So it is that a word from a heart that is not Spirit cleansed can cause power failure. A man was visiting a large factory where hundreds of looms were spinning. The manager of the mill told the visitor that the machinery was so delicate that if a single thread out of thirty thousand were to break, all of the looms would instantly stop. He proceeded to break a thread to illustrate his point. Immediately every loom stopped until the thread was rejoined. Some word of ours may have broken the prayer communication, and it will take repentance to restore it to operation.

Our acts, too, are the product of our thoughts. We need to check them as a source of power failures. Did we maneuver into the check-out line at the supermarket ahead of some other customer? Did we take a few berries out of this basket and add them to another?

---

[10]Pr. 23:7.

Wilfred Grenfell, once a missionary doctor in Labrador, received a new motorboat from some friends in England to aid him in his work. The very night the boat arrived he was called to visit a sick woman desperately ill on one of the ice-bound islands. Fighting this way through icy seas, carefully following the compass of his new boat, he suddenly realized he was lost. Hours passed in the frigid darkness before he found his way to the tiny island he sought, only to find that the woman had died. There was reason to believe her life might have been saved if he had arrived earlier.

When the boat was checked to determine the cause of the compass malfunction, it was discovered that way back in England a careless workman had used a steel screw instead of a brass one to mount the compass. A "brassy" word or deed may be as disastrous a cause of power failure in our lives.

Lest we be discouraged at the possibility of our daily lives gendering so many hindrances to prayer, let's remember that we need not be so troubled, for we have an all-powerful God who keeps the Holy Spirit on duty twenty-four hours a day as a trouble shooter.

In our telephone books is a section that says, "To report trouble. . . ." God says the same thing: "If we confess our sins, he is faithful and just to forgive us our sins, and to cleanse us from all unrighteousness."[11]

---

[11] 1 Jn. 1:9.

Confession presupposes repentance, which has been well defined as a change of heart with a corresponding change of action. Power failure cannot be corrected without repentance.

In some areas of our country there still remain a few old mills operated by a water wheel. Once these wheels turned machinery to grind corn. Suppose the river that turned the wheel became clogged with dead branches and other debris. The wheel would stop and could not be started turning again until that which clogged it was removed. The sins of our minds, tongues, hearts, and hands have to be removed by repentance before the power failure can be corrected and the wheels of prayer can turn again. Organizations and programs and plans won't alter matters. Only repentance can restore the power flow.

It has been said that the reason David was a man after God's own heart was that he was such a ready repenter. Repentance calls for a tender heart. Maybe we need to ask God to give us hearts sensitive to sin, tender enough to repent quickly of the seemingly trivial things that are causing power failure and hindering our prayers.

Not long ago there were two tragedies in Japan. In one, 452 men were killed in a mine explosion. In another 162 persons perished in a train wreck. Investigation showed that both calamities resulted from a faulty cotter pin, maybe not more than an inch long.

We may regard many of the items in our life as nothing more than a cotter pin, but let's remember that trifles can wreck lives. Let's keep in mind that pencil marks, beverage cans, or broken threads can bring power failure.

Solomon said, "The little foxes spoil the vines."[12] Notice that he didn't say the elephants or the rhinos but the baby foxes. And it may be the little foxes (sins) that are tangling up our prayer lines and interrupting communication between us and our Lord. "But the trouble is that your sins have cut you off from God. Because of sin he has turned his face away from you and will not listen anymore."[13]

Because prayer produces the most satisfying outcomes and the most gratifying achievements of all the activities in which a Christian might engage, he simply cannot afford to tolerate prayer failure. He must reestablish contact with his Power Source.

---

[12]S. of S. 2:15.   [13]Isa. 59:2, TLB.

ABOMINABLE
PRAYER

"He that turneth away his ear from hearing the law; even his prayer shall be abomination."[1]

The force of the original Hebrew for abomination is "disgusting" or "loathesome." Among other items described as abominable in the Bible are filth, lewdness, unclean animals, idolatry, whoredom, etc. You can see, therefore, in what class your prayers fall if they are prayed while you are flouting God's law and disregarding his commandments. It may be wise to examine possible specific disobediences that may be "grounding" or "short-circuiting" your prayers.

Unforgiveness or *grudge-holding* is one likely factor. "But when you are praying, first forgive anyone you are holding a grudge against, so that your Father in heaven will forgive you your sins too."[2]

The grudge one is carrying may be based on an actual mistreatment. He may unquestionably have been wronged; nevertheless, unforgiveness is a luxury he cannot afford. It has been well said that "nothing will get you so out of step with

---

[1]Pr. 28:9. [2]Mk. 11:25, TLB.

God, and so at cross-purposes, as a lack of forgiveness . . . To prevail in prayer, and to be mighty with God in the fulfillment of his promises, we must be right with our fellowmen . . . Though it may hurt like the pulling of all your teeth, you must forgive; or give up the hope of becoming an effective intercessor."[3]

In Reformation times some persecuted followers of Huss, Luther, and Calvin found themselves thrown together by circumstances on the estate of wealthy Count Zinzendorf. There were many items of belief on which they did not agree, and it would have been easy for them to give way to bickering and quarreling, thus stunting the spiritual development of each, and hindering their prayers.

Instead, they drew up a covenant to "seek out and emphasize the points on which they agreed" rather than their differences of opinion. As a result of this attitude they became a blessing to each other and prevailed in prayer through the unity of the Spirit.

As a result of the work of the Spirit, a native pastor who attended a World Vision Pastors' Conference was convicted that his own pride and stubbornness had contributed to the proliferation of a contention between two groups. After repenting and confessing his fault he became a key man in bringing about a reconciliation. No doubt prayer was a factor.

In another situation a Christian reported that

---

[3]J. F. Huegel, *Herald of His Coming*, Nov. 1970.

he had prayed for years for the conversion of an erring son but the youth only seemed to go from bad to worse. The man confesses that all the time he was praying he had a resentful attitude toward a brother who he felt had wronged him and from whom he demanded reparation, but without response.

Finally, the father was convicted that his bitterness was hindering the answer to his prayer for his son. When he got right with God it was not long until he received word that the young man, far from home at the time, had come under the influence of the gospel and been saved.

As one has said, "We cannot dynamite our way through to God if we harbor a grudge against any living soul, or hold an unforgiving spirit against any creature whatsoever."[4]

Quarrels between husband and wife which engender resentment and ill-will not only stifle the spirit of prayer and render one unfit to pray, but may also constitute a hindrance to answered prayer. They are nearly always accompanied by selfishness, pride, judging, and other corollary sins which are known from Scripture to interfere with effective prayer.

"You husbands must be careful of your wives, being thoughtful of their needs and honoring them as the weaker sex. Remember that you and your wife are partners in receiving God's blessings, and if you don't treat her as you should, your prayers will not get ready answers."[5]

---

[4]*Herald of His Coming*, June 1971.   [5] Pet. 3:7, TLB.

This verse is addressed to husbands, but applies equally to wives.

A husband and wife were daydreaming over plans for a new home which was not as yet even in the drawing board stage. In the plans they were inspecting there was a small room in the basement not designated for any particular function.

"I'll make a little workshop of it," the husband projected. "I can put in a bench with a little lathe and stuff and do carpentry and woodwork there."

"Why you don't have time for anything like that! You wouldn't use it once a month," the wife replied. "It's just right for a sewing room. I've already made up my mind to fit it up that way."

That night both of them tossed and turned in bed, each thinking resentfully of the selfishness of the other. At breakfast they were politely cool to each other. The husband left without giving his wife the customary kiss. All day she pouted and felt abused that he would even entertain the idea of commandeering the coveted space.

Just after the husband's return from work that evening, with coolness still evident on the part of both, the telephone rang. The husband answered.

"It's Debbie Waters," he turned to his wife and explained. "Her father has been critically injured in a car wreck. Her mother wants us to pray for him."

Brother Waters was the minister who had married them, and they were both very fond of him. With common consent they dropped to their knees but neither one prayed audibly. After a moment of tension the husband said, "Well, go ahead and pray."

"Dear God," the wife began, and then stopped.

"Heavenly Father," the husband finally began, and then he, too, stopped.

"We can't pray acceptably, feeling as we do," the wife melted, and began to cry.

"Lord, forgive us . . ." said the husband.

"You can have the room for a shop," the wife interrupted in tearful repentance.

"Heavenly Father," the husband began again, "forgive us our foolishness. We want to pray for Brother Waters. . . ."

Then there is the prayer hindrance of doubt. It is not often regarded as disobedience to God. We are inclined to rationalize that it is natural and excusable rather than blameworthy. But the Bible says, "Have faith in God,"[6] therefore to lack faith is to disobey God. The Scripture expressly states, "Without faith it is impossible to please him for he that cometh to God must believe that he is, and that he is a rewarder of them that diligently seek him."[7]

One man of Bible record cried out, "Lord, I believe; help thou mine unbelief."[8] The apostles prayed, "Lord, increase our faith."[9] We can follow these examples and pray for our own un-

---

[6]Mk. 11:22. [7]Heb. 11:6. [8]Mk. 9:24. [9]Lu. 17:5.

belief to be reversed and the little faith we have to be expanded. We can use Bible study to that end. Wavering is just a form of doubt, and is abominable in prayer.[10]

To pray lightly and superficially is also a violation of God's commands. Both Elijah and Christ are recorded as praying *earnestly*. Dare we pray otherwise? Unfortunately, we do. We brashly rush into God's presence with untimely, ill-considered requests: "Father, do this . . ." "God, give me that . . .", without having the Spirit's endorsement of what we ask.

Or we mouth sanctimonious-sounding entreaties such as, "Lord, save the lost in this service today," when we couldn't care less. In fact, we hadn't cared enough about the lost to invite one to be present.

God has not promised to honor insincere petitions. He has warned, "When you pray, don't be like the hypocrites. . . ."[11]

The promise is, "He is close to all who call on him sincerely."[12]

We are reminded of the man who regularly prayed in the midweek services, "O Lord, fill me. Fill me with thy Spirit." Finally his worn-down wife cried out, "Don't you do it, Lord. He leaks!" Probably our spouses are better able than any other human being to judge the sincerity of our prayers, but of course God knows positively and accurately how sincere they are.

The prayer of an idolater is abomination to

---

[10]Jas. 1:6, 7.   [11]Matt. 6:5, TLB.   [12]Ps. 145:18, TLB.

God. "Well," you shrug, "idolaters are the heathen in Asia or the pagan in Africa who worship images. We don't have any here." Not so — an idolater is one who places anyone or anything ahead of God. He has given priority in his life to his family, his career, his hobby, his car or boat, his image of himself.

A certain Christian homemaker gave priority to her home. Its beauty became her god. She put off her daughter's request to help with doll clothes because she was absorbed with draperies. She discouraged her son from bringing his friends home because they would track up her polished floors. She failed to share her husband's business interests and problems because she preferred to be planning decorator touches for her home.

The years passed and finally the day came when her lovely home was all she had. Everyone had left, and she was alone. At last she realized her folly and confessed it to God in prayer asking him to fill her empty life with love for him and others. Of course he did.

The Scripture warns, "Son of dust, these men worship idols in their hearts — should I let them ask me anything?"[13]

Not long ago a newspaper item told of a Yoruban tribal king's effort to alter the deplorable lack of sanitation in the capital city. He set aside a day for the people to pray for relief from their clogged drains, dirty streets, and disease-spreading sewers.

---

[13]Ez. 14:3, TLB.

The next day the streets were the same as before the prayer proclamation. The explanation was twofold: no one "put feet on his prayers" by making an effort to clean up the streets. In fact, few prayed, for according to the king, pleasure was the god of the people and revelry was all that interested them.

Any sin can defeat our prayers because it separates us from God. "If I regard iniquity in my heart, the Lord will not hear me."[14]

Perhaps it is in order at this point to catechize ourselves about our prayer practices. The following questions may help us to recognize where they need correcting.

1. Have I had the attitude that I was doing God a favor by praying?

2. Have I blamed him for my unanswered prayers? Could I be the one who is to blame?

3. Have I checked my daily life to see if anything in it accounts for my prayer failures?

4. Do I examine my motives as I pray?

5. How wide is the field of my prayers?

6. Do I pray only for family? friends? fellow-citizens? Caucasians?

7. Do I pray only about "big" things or about "little ones," too?

8. Are thanksgiving and praise part of my prayers?

9. Can I detect growth in my prayer life?

10. Do I regard prayer as a last resort? a gamble? a duty? a privilege?

---

[14]Ps. 66:18.

11. How long has it been since I've had a prayer answered?

12. Do I commune with God or just give him a list of wants? Would a recording do as well?

13. Do I recognize the role of Christ and the Holy Spirit in prayer?

14. Have I based my prayer requests and expectations on the Word of God?

15. Do I ever make a Bible study of prayer, its principles and examples?

In the answers to these questions we may find the key to whether or not our prayers are abominable to God.

CROWDING OUT
PRAYER

It is easy to think of consequences of neglect: what happened to a child, a friendship, a piece of machinery, a building, a tool, or even a tooth, because someone put off or neglected the needed ministry. Yet the worst instance that you can recall does not compare with the seriousness of prayer neglect because the unaccomplished things of life, the undone achievements of the world, the unembraced opportunities of Christendom can be attributed to failure to pray.

One has said, "There is not a vile sin in the world but what prayerlessness is a part of it, and that real prayerfulness would not have prevented or cured it. Of itself prayerlessness is, I have no doubt, worse than murder, worse than adultery, worse than blasphemy. It is more fundamental. It more clearly reveals the heart."[1]

Most Christians do not willfully neglect prayer, yet neither can they claim to do it ignorantly. They are aware of its tremendous possibilities, of the need, of the urgency to pray, yet they fail to pray because they let it be crowded out.

---

[1]*Prayer—Asking and Receiving*, John R. Rice.

Like the servant in the prophet's allegory[2] who was "busy here and there" and let a prisoner escape, so God's people get busy with this and that and let prayer opportunities and obligations escape. *To do so is sin.*

Prayerlessness is sin because God's Word so defines it. Samuel said, "Moreover, as for me, far be it from me that I should sin against the Lord by ceasing to pray for you. . . ."[3]

Prayerlessness is sin because it is disobedience to God. The Bible exhortations to pray are too many to cite. Everyone is aware of them, but most people ignore them. Most of the time people use prayer only as the airman does a parachute: for an emergency.

Prayerlessness is sin because it deprives one of the peace of mind and freedom from anxiety which God meant for him to have. "Stop being worried about anything, but always in prayer and entreaty, and with thanksgiving keep on making your wants known to God. Then through your union with Christ Jesus, the peace of God, that surpasses all human thought, will keep guard over your hearts and thoughts."[4]

A middle-aged woman engaged in sales work was subject to so much pressure that she felt she must seek a different place of employment. On her lunch time she tried to telephone about a position advertised in the newspaper. Invariably she got the busy signal. With her noon hour nearly gone, her frustrations caused tension to

---

[2]1 Kg. 20:39, 40.   [3]1 Sam. 12:23.   [4]Phil. 4:6, 7, Williams.

mount. Then the Lord seemed to say to her, "Have you forgotten me?"

She was convicted that she had done so momentarily, so she confessed her sin and asked for guidance. Calm permeated her and she returned to work relaxed and in good spirits. That afternoon she qualified for a bonus. Upon arriving home she found in the mail a summons to jury duty. That would relieve her of job pressure for a month. The next day she received a phone call from a place where she had worked some years previously. An interview resulted in part-time employment while she was on jury duty and full-time work when it was over. Her initial fretfulness and failure to pray illustrate the lines from a familiar hymn:

> "Oh, what peace we often forefeit,
> Oh, what needless pain we bear,
> All because we do not carry
> Everything to God in prayer."

Prayer is truly God's medium for communicating peace in troubled times. A missionary to China gives a dramatic testimony of the perils through which God preserved a group of them. They had been told to leave their field and were waiting in Yengchow for a plane to take them out. It never arrived, and meanwhile the Communists mounted an offensive against the city.

In the course of enemy shelling they had many a narrow escape. Despite repeated attacks the missionaries were spared even a scratch, though shells pitted the walls except the silhouette outlined by one missionary's body. (The women were under the bed.) Dead and dying lay all around outside.

One missionary afterwards wrote, "Never before had I experienced such a feeling of peace and strength as I did that day . . . The greatest miracle of all those days was the peace of heart that I felt in the midst of great danger."[5]

It was a peace mediated through prayer.

Prayerlessness is sin because it is spurning to co-work with God. "But you must help us too, by praying for us. For much thanks and praise will go to God from you who see his wonderful answers to your prayers for our safety!"[6]

A woman who found herself wakeful in the middle of the night used to pray during that period. One night, wearying of prayer, she begged the Lord to favor her with sleep and cited, ". . . for so he giveth his beloved sleep."[7]

It seemed to her as if the Lord replied, "Oh! You'd rather sleep than talk to me!"

She was crushed by the thought. Since then she has tried to utilize wakeful times in prayer, trusting that, "he knoweth our frame; he remembereth that we are dust,"[8] and that if she really needs sleep he will see that she gets it. Moreover, night hours afford a better opportunity for prayer than most others because of freedom from distraction, because of the quiet and still-

---

[5]Reported in *Commission*, June 1958.   [6]2 Cor. 1:11, TLB.
[7]Ps. 127:2.   [8]Ps. 103:14.

ness of the period, and the aloneness with the Lord.[9]

Prayerlessness is sin because it is omission. "Remember that knowing what is right to do and then not doing it is sin."[10] Few earnest Christians have escaped the smiting of conscience for failure to pray. Some grievous event occurs and he recalls, *I never prayed for that one's safety,* or *I failed to pray about that situation,* etc.

Prayerlessness is sin because it contributes to unfulfillment of God's purposes. ". . . ye have not because ye ask not."[11] God meant for his children to have an abundant life. Man desires it, too, and even fights for it, as the cited Scripture sets forth, and yet he does not use God's appointed means of obtaining what he wants.

Moreover, he deprives himself and others of assistance that might have been theirs if he had used his prayer privilege and opportunity. Think for a minute about instances of this in your own life.

You were frustrated because of that misplaced item, but did you ask the Lord to help you find it? You were anxious about your husband's business deal but did you discuss it with God? You were fearful that your son was not mature enough for the activities he was choosing. Did you entreat the Father to guide his planning?

---

[9]The medical profession has pointed out that the unconsciousness of slumber is not always needed to revitalize one, that rest and relaxation may be equally effective. [10]Jas. 4:17.   [11]Jas. 4:2.

You had two engagements develop for the same date. Did you ask God to resolve the conflict for you?

Think over your present difficulties and see how many you have tried to handle yourself instead of asking God's assistance. Do the same about others (even strangers) who you know have unmet needs or unsolved problems. Consider whether or not you have asked blessings for them through prayer. Has your indifference or neglect been a sin of silence?

Prayerlessness is sin because it fosters friction and tension. This fact is stressed in the passage already cited. If one would only pray, much for which he fights and struggles would be taken care of without his becoming embroiled. In this way he cheats himself, because God meant for him to have the satisfaction of co-working with God on a given project, and the thrill of prayer being answered regarding it, but by not praying he forfeits both.

Prayerlessness is sin because it is failure to profit by the examples and experiences of other children of God. Jesus himself, also the apostles and a host of Old and New Testament persons engaged in prayer. An unknown writer has called attention to the fact that Moses was a praying leader, Elijah a praying prophet, Hezekiah a praying king, Ezra a praying reformer, Nehemiah a praying builder, Daniel a praying captive, Hannah a praying mother, Esther a praying queen, and Lydia a praying business woman. Inasmuch as their experiences were preserved for our edification,[12] then to whatever extent we ignore them, we have frustrated the purposes of God.

Finally, prayerlessness is sin because it may be indicative of an utterly backslidden condition. Isaiah voices God's indictment of such in these words: "And there is none that calleth upon thy name, that stirreth up himself to take hold of thee: for thou hast hid thy face from us and hast consumed us, because of our iniquities."[13]

You may have seen a parent take hold of a child and say, "Now you listen to me . . ." but have you ever been so in earnest that you "took hold of God"?

We hear people on street corners or university campuses or broadcasts who are stirred up about one thing and another and want to take hold of the government or society about it, but how often do we hear anyone trying desperately to take hold of God because of the separation caused by sin? How often and how recently have you been stirred up to try to take hold of God about anything?

The usual thought one has in regard to prayerlessness is that he doesn't have time to do more praying. "I have to be on the job . . ." "I have to go here or there . . ." "I have meals to get . . ." and so on.

True enough, and God planned and expects you to be diligent regarding your responsibilities, but as someone has pointed out, to say you

---

[12]1 Cor. 10:11.   [13]Isa. 64:7.

haven't time to pray is like saying you don't have time to breathe. People get alarmed over lack of oxygen or vitamin deficiency, yet they may be indifferent to a prayer shortage which is equally serious.

Moreover, prayer can be engaged in simultaneously with many activities. One can pray as he drives to work (maybe instead of listening to the radio or stereo tapes). One can pray while ironing (rather than watching television soap operas). Besides that, God will reveal to the one who desires it earnestly, how he can sandwich prayer between obligations or before them. Some churches in the Orient schedule their weekly prayer meetings at five A.M. Many a saint of God has sacrificed sleep to keep an early morning tryst with God. A man greatly used of God, F. B. Meyer, prayed, "In my religious life may the neglect of prayer and thy Holy Word be things of the past. Wake me morning by morning to hear as a disciple. Enable me to spring up at thy call, and like all thy true servants, to rise up early in the morning to gather the manna ere the dew be gone from it."

If we don't *make* time for prayer, our heavenly Father, out of love, may compel us to *take* time for it in bed or hospital or with the unemployed on a park bench. It may even be dangerous not to pray. David confessed, "Before I was afflicted I went astray; but now have I kept thy word."[14]

---

[14]Ps. 119:67.

How much more pleasant it is to pray voluntarily than to have it wrung from us by discipline! Actually there is nothing as important in life as praying. Other activities produce what *we* can do. Prayer's output is what *God* can do.

BE DARING
IN PRAYER

We read with interest reports of adventurers
who travel ocean lanes in a sailboat, or intrepid
speleologists who explore caves, or courageous
climbers who scale steep mountain peaks. The
same daring can be invested in prayer, and that
without physical hazard, special gear, or distant
sojourn. Moreover, it can be exercised lying on
a bed, sitting in a car, standing in a shower stall,
kneeling in a chapel, or jogging in a park.

How wonderful that the handicapped, disabled,
infirm, or aged are not excluded from it! How
thrilling that it is just as much the opportunity
and responsibility of the young as the mature!
Prayer is the most economical investment (money-
wise) and the most convenient endeavor (body-
wise) of all pursuits available to man. How exciting that absolutely anyone, anywhere, may
engage in it! Therefore pray *ye*.

Be daring about the span of your prayers. Don't
confine yourself to your county, state, or even
your nation. Let the earth be your prayer beat —
yea, beyond that, into space. Be as challenged
by the scope of prayer as Adoniram Judson was.
As he lay on his death bed he read that some

Jews in Turkey had been saved by reading of his sufferings in Burma. Then he remembered that as a youth he had prayed to go to Jerusalem. He was overcome by the reach of his ministry.

Keep in mind that there is no ethnological limitation on prayer. You can pray for any race or nationality, for a person of any culture or folkway. A missionary in Japan was about to participate in a Bible camp. She mailed letters to friends in America requesting prayer for a fruitful session.

The first few days of the camp were not unusual, but on the fourth day things began to happen. Several were saved, and testified to the change and joy it brought into their lives. One confessed to despair and suicidal impulses.

The missionary calculated that her prayer requests would have been received by the American intercessors on that fourth day. She was able to praise God for what she believed they had wrought by their prayers.[1]

Civic organizations and local projects might well be matters of prayer. There was a move in a community to liberalize liquor laws. It became a prayer concern of individuals and churches. The measure was defeated. In another instance, a couple noticed a tavern being constructed beside the highway they followed to town. They prayed that it would not be permitted to operate in their area, but they did not communicate with anyone about it. Midway to completion, construction

---

[1] Reported in *Horizons*, July/August 1971.

stopped. They did not hear why, but they thanked the Lord. To this day the half-finished building stands as a testimony to answered prayer.

Even a club program, to say nothing of a church program, may be a challenge to daring prayer. A secular institution scheduled a speaker that a parent did not feel would be edifying to the youth who would hear him. Sharing his concern only with the Lord, he was thrilled to learn of the cancellation of the address, due to "unavoidable circumstances."

Had there been more prayer all along about ecology, natural resources and their use, there might be less need of concern about them today. We may well pray about them on a national, regional, or household basis. What kind of regulations should the government impose for waste disposal? Should a dam be built across Crooked Creek? Must I forego my favorite enzyme soak? All such matters are suitable prayer material.

Every newscast should be a challenge to daring prayer. Is there a cholera epidemic in the Orient? Has there been a typhoon or tidal wave on the islands of the sea? a plane or train wreck on the east or west coast? Think of all that is involved in such an event: removal and identification of bodies, autopsies, shock to survivors or bereaved, pinpointing of blame on human error or mechanical failure (some Christian's future may be involved here) and much more. Compassion should compel prayer.

The health and welfare of individuals can always be an exciting adventure in prayer. A missionary's national driver had a wife who was emotionally disturbed. She would seem like one person on one occasion and then would unexplainably change completely with even the tone of her voice changing. American psychiatrists might have diagnosed it as a split personality.

Prayer had been offered by various individuals, but when the woman's condition worsened, a few of the most concerned assembled, with her present, to intercede definitely for her. The result was that she was completely delivered from her affliction.

Marital friction should stimulate prayer. In a given church there was a seasoned Christian and his newly saved wife who were about to separate. It became a matter of discreet church prayer. Many were expecting the man to respond to the Spirit's leading and separate himself from the divorce action. As it turned out, it was the wife who took the initiative in the reconciliation, but the hearts of all who had prayed were warmed to see their prayers answered.

Seeing social needs met through prayer is exciting. A handicapped spinster, who had to get about the house in a wheelchair, lived by herself after her mother died. Neighbors and church friends were interested in her and kept a watch over her. The welfare department made regular visits and gave her assistance.

Gradually, however, she withdrew from people, spent more and more time in bed, and became somewhat crotchety. Corollary to this, her house became more and more ill kept and even unsanitary. She stubbornly refused to be transferred to a home where she would have proper care and food.

Prayer was offered by those who feared for her health and safety. At length she yielded to persuasion and was installed in a convalescent home, where she soon came to enjoy her surroundings. What pressure could not accomplish, prayer had. A special factor in a situation like that is that one can have a part through prayer without being meddlesome or without running the risk of being considered a busybody.

The area of emotional needs is another in which prayer can bring thrilling results. A young married woman who needed some surgery on her teeth had an abnormal fear and dread of the ordeal. She assumed it would be better for her to go to the hospital for it, but she could visualize all kinds of complications and crises.

So great was her emotional involvement over the matter that she kept delaying going to the dentist to make arrangements. She kept praying for the Lord to strengthen her and give her courage, but her tension was high.

Finally she got herself to the dentist's office to consult with him, but she was trembling with apprehension. She explained her condition to the dentist, and he assured her the matter could be safely and satisfactorily taken care of in his office. As he talked, he told her, "You're just going to have to trust me."

Instantly it crossed her mind that this was exactly what God was telling her. With the thought came a great peace of mind that she could do just that. She testified that it was an answer to prayer that she had been delivered from the frenzied emotions which had been gripping her.

There was a pastor's wife who was a very reticent person, shy and suffering from an inferiority complex. She dreaded being around people because she felt she had nothing to offer them. Yet she realized that her attitudes were a hindrance to her husband and to the Lord's work. Therefore she earnestly prayed that the Lord would change her personality.

In the course of time the Lord did that very thing for her. Instead of being an introvert she became an outgoing person. She developed a listening ear which many troubled persons used because they felt she would be sympathetic to their trials or their triumphs.

Her personality change was recognized by both parishioners and friends, some of whom commented, "Why, she is just a different person!" which was just what she had prayed for.

Several instances of prayer for material needs being answered have already been cited. Such intercession is not merely an exercise in logistics such as getting surplus provisions to someone who needs them, with God making the arrangements, although sometimes it seems almost that simple.

A children's home in Oklahoma, which operated on a faith basis, had to provide two thousand meals a week for the residents. Sometimes supplies were exhausted and their only resource was prayer. On one such occasion, when there was no visible basis for expectation, a man whom they had never seen before appeared at the door with three thousand frozen chickens. He offered them with the simple statement, "I want to help a little," and left without identifying himself.

In another state a wife on a very limited budget had come to the place of badly needing a frock for dress-up wear. Before leaving home she asked the Lord to direct her where to shop and what to choose. She prayed he would provide her with a dress she could afford and that she would enjoy wearing.

As she entered a store where she expected to look at dresses she saw one in the window that attracted her, but at once she saw that the price was beyond her means. As she was making her way to the dress department she passed a table of ready-to-wear items that had been marked down. Among them she spied a duplicate of the dress in the window!

Upon examining it she discovered that the zipper was jammed, which probably accounted for the price reduction. As she stood there praying and fiddling with the slide it suddenly came unjammed and operated properly. She never doubted but that the Lord arranged the matter for her benefit.

Years ago on a certain mission field there was a state of famine. The Christians gathered daily to pray for relief, though they had no source from which to expect it except God. One day a dark cloud was sighted on the horizon. Suddenly it began to rain heavily, but it was no ordinary downpour. What fell proved to be edible grain in sufficient quantity to keep the people alive until harvest, which would be about a month later. It was learned that a great storm had wrecked a grain depository, and the seeds had been carried fifteen hundred miles by the wind. Who could question but that it was in answer to earnest prayer?

There are even exciting answers to prayer in the political realm. A tense situation existed in a foreign country where missionaries were stationed. Factions to the left and to the right were struggling for control. The missionaries prayed much about it but were very careful not to identify themselves with either group, though of course they favored the anticommunist forces. When a leftist coup d'etat failed because of certain fortuitous circumstances, the missionaries knew that their steadfast prayer had been heard.

People seem to marvel less about answered prayer for spiritual matters than for any other type, and they are usually inclined to view them as scarcely to be classified as exciting. But what could be any more exciting than incidents such as this one:

"I've taken the message to Greenland, covered with ice and snow and glaciers, and men have found Christ, because of this Book. I have taken this Book all over Europe and have seen men find Christ. I've taken this Book to Vietnam and stood out on muddy hillsides and I've seen rough, tough men with grenades pinned to their lapels and rifles slung across their shoulders, break down and weep because Christ had come into their lives.

"I have had men nineteen and twenty years old come and see me with glassy, staring eyes, sometimes their eyes running with tears, their nose running and saliva dripping from their mouth, because they hadn't had a fix of heroin and they were ready to kill someone to get a fix. And Christ healed them! And that is the power of this Word!"[2]

And no doubt the military chaplain who thus testifies could have added that prayer was the pad from which every ministry of the Word was launched.

There was a national seminary student in the Orient who was an eloquent preacher but did not lead a life which was consistent with his profession. Much prayer was offered about his need to repent and change. Seminary officials dealt with him regarding it but apparently without effect. Eventually, due to prayer pressure, the erring Christian was deeply convicted and publicly confessed his sins, asking for forgiveness. Even those who did not know what had taken place were impressed with the difference in him, and they commented on it.

A church treasurer, a national on a foreign field, and a very poor man, yielded to temptation and embezzled church funds. The local church was aware of his defection and prayed earnestly

---

[2]Reported in *The Gideon*, Sept. 1971.

about it. As a result of their prayers the man repented and asked forgiveness publicly, promising to make restitution. An unsaved man who witnessed the man's confession was so impressed that he accepted Christ and offered to help the man make restitution.

Obviously there is no area in life in which prayer cannot make a difference.

We think nothing of it when we read in the paper that the governor of a certain state could with one finger put into operation a great irrigation project consisting of twenty-one dams with a capacity of nearly seven million acre feet of water which will flow to one hundred twenty cities. We accept without any credibility gap the fact that the system's eighty-thousand-horsepower pumps will discharge one hundred fifty gallons of water a minute, pumping it over mountains two thousand feet high and along a two hundred eighty five mile distance.

We note without astonishment that all the governor had to do to start this system operating was press a button. If one individual can initiate such a culmination of engineering skill, why do we question what one person might do through prayer?

We marvel at the "miracles" achieved by modern science. For instance, there is the laser beam. A helium neon laser can measure the distance between two atoms — one one-thousandth of one-millionth of an inch! It can detect how much movement has occurred if we take two points ten thousand miles apart and move one a fraction of the thickness of a human hair. Or the laser tracking system can pinpoint within twelve inches the exact location of a rapidly moving object up to a height of eight miles.

Another marvel is the guided missile, which can traverse space and has within itself the means for controlling its flight so it can detect a target, determine its position, classify its kind, and destroy it. Still another marvel is the transmission by telephone of an electrocardiogram, permitting a doctor three thousand miles away to hear the heartbeat of a patient.

Why do we have faith in guided missiles and not in prayer? Why do we spend billions of dollars for the one, but won't so much as bow the head or bend the knee for the other?

Prayer has all the possibilities of a laser or a missile, either literally or figuratively. By it we can transmit our heartbeat to God. We can indicate to him a certain satanic target that must be detected and destroyed. We can give him the location or identity of a need, and from outer space he can set forces in operation to meet it. Prayer procures a direct connection with the greatest power in the universe.

Nothing is impossible![3] *All things are possible!*[4]

Therefore pray *ye* because prayer is practical, prudent, productive — and *exciting!*

---

[3]Matt. 17:20.   [4]Matt. 19:26.

God probably appreciates spontaneous, informal prayer more than eloquent phraseology or "prepared statements" such as interviewed persons sometimes give on broadcasts. Since prayer is simply conversation with God, one should scarcely need any sort of pattern or formulated paragraphs to use in praying. Yet some persons are not talkative by nature or are as yet inexperienced in prayer, consequently they would welcome suggestions and guidance.

The following prayer "samples" afford opportunities for insertion of personal details. It is to be hoped that every child of God can quickly become so accustomed to talking everything over with his Father through prayer that he can soon "throw away the script" and "ad lib" about his needs and those of others, and about the areas in which he hopes God will work.

God may be addressed in whatever term seems most natural and appropriate to you. One person always opens his prayer with, "Holy and Righteous Father," another with "Heavenly Father," still another with "Dear God" or only "Lord." Jesus in the model prayer suggested, "Our Father." Choose the name or salutation which best expresses your adoration, appreciation, trust, and closeness to him.

Don't forget praise and thanksgiving. It is a good way to open any prayer, either for general blessings or specific items.

Be mindful of the importance of a clear conscience.[1] If you recognize sin in your life, repent and confess it before you attempt to ask anything.[2]

It promotes confidence to have a promise of God from his Word to plead, and the more specifically it seems to relate to the prayer matter, the more helpful it seems to be in offering effective prayer.

The foregoing suggestions are for your benefit, not God's. Of the prayers which follow, only the first one is for those who are not members of God's family by faith in Jesus Christ.

Prayer for a Right Relationship with God

Holy and Righteous God:

I want to be right with you. I want to be able to pray expectantly, to know that I am your child, and that I have a right to pray in the Holy Spirit using Jesus' name, with each of them interceding for me.

Help me to bare my heart to you and open it to Christ. Convict me of my own utter unworthiness and inability to approach you on the basis of my own merit. Enable me through Jesus Christ

---

[1]Ps. 66:18; 1 Jn. 3:1. [2]1 Jn. 1:9.

to have faith and believe in you. Prompt me to discard all reliance on myself, and put all my trust in what Christ did for me on the cross. Lead me to approach you by the only way open to me.

Right now deliver me from the power of sin, from separation from you, and from everlasting condemnation. Accept me into your family because of my belief in the shed blood of the Lord Jesus Christ as the sacrifice for my sin.

I thank you that I can be born anew right now, that I can receive everlasting life, membership in God's family, and be a new creature from this moment forth.

I do in faith receive Jesus as my personal Savior, and it is now in his name I pray.

[You may wish, and would do well, to go ahead and commit your whole way of life to him at this time also, receiving Christ not only as your Savior, but also as your Sovereign.]

Prayer for Fellowship

Heavenly Father:

I feel the need of human companionship.

[Fill in the specific need you feel, someone to share your blessings, to dissipate your loneliness, accompany you on outings, cooperate on social projects, even be your life partner.]

Lord, the Bible says, "God setteth the solitary in families,"[3] and indicates that you endorse fel-

---

[3]Ps. 68:6.

lowship, that you even counsel about it, that you also approve of marriage in the Lord, so I come asking you to arrange for this need of mine to be met. Help me to think in terms of what I might do for another to bless him, not merely in respect to what he might do for me.

Cause the Spirit to reveal to me anything I need to do for myself [as in personal hygiene or grooming] or opportunities I am rejecting that would afford fellowship [such as participating in church activities]. Deliver me from carnal conniving [such as lonely hearts clubs, etc.] where Satan might capitalize on my yearnings or maneuver me into bringing reproach on your name.

In the meantime, help me to experience increasing joy day by day, in fellowship with you.

In Jesus' name I pray.

Prayer for Forgiveness and Cleansing

Dear Lord:

I come before you, as an erring child of yours, in need of forgiveness for this sin:

> [Spell it out. Be specific. Don't gloss over the circumstances or rationalize or alibi about your guilt.]

Lord, help me to realize how evil it is in your sight, even if men know nothing about it, or would not condemn me if they did. As David said, "Against thee, thee only have I sinned, and done this evil in thy sight."[4]

---

[4] Ps. 51:4.

Lord, convict me of how I have grieved you first of all, plus the effect it may have had on others.

[Rehearse to God how you may have failed another or wronged him or caused him to stumble.]

I pray, as did David, "Create in me a clean heart, O God, and renew a right spirit within me."[5]

I thank you, Lord, that you have promised, "If we confess our sins, he is faithful and just to forgive us our sins, and to cleanse us from all unrighteousness."[6]

I accept your forgiveness and cleansing and ask you to help me not to repeat this sin.

In Jesus' name I pray.

Prayer for Guidance

Dear Lord:

I am a confused child of yours and I am uncertain about which way to go. I come asking to be guided into that direction which is your will for my life. I do not know whether to. . . .

[Explain the courses that are open to you. God does not need this information, he already has it, but it will clarify matters in your own mind, and help you to discern his leading, if you lay the alternatives out before him.]

Lord, please convict me of those possibilities which may be contrary to your word and will.

---

[5]Ps. 51:10.   [6]1 Jn. 1:9.

Give me grace to eliminate them from my choices even if they look attractive to me.

Lord, you have said, "If any of you lack wisdom, let him ask of God, that giveth to all men liberally, and upbraideth not, and it shall be given him."[7] That promise justifies my expecting guidance from you. You have said, "And thine ear shall hear a voice behind thee saying, This is the way, walk ye in it."[8] Give me sensitiveness to hear your voice, and patience to stand still until I do.

In Jesus' name I pray.

Prayer for Career Success

Dear Lord:

Your word records how you endued men with skill for specific projects,[9] so I come to you now asking help in respect to my work. . . .

[Spread out the details of your need before him, such as ability to perform a particular task, or strength to put in a certain number of hours, or personality to manage employees satisfactorily, or finesse to cope with a difficult situation, or whatever you desire.]

Father, I do not pray for advantage to myself alone, but for ability to contribute to the advantage of all concerned. Purify my motive in every respect. Also, Lord, if it should be that I am not now in your choice of vocation or job, then

---

[7]Jas. 1:5.   [8]Isa. 30:21.   [9]Ex. 35:30-35.

show me that fact, and arrange a changeover to what is your will for me.

You know, God, those who are dependent upon me. Enable me to meet their needs, but keep me mindful that all I have, or receive, is yours, that I am only a steward of it, and that I therefore owe you, first of all, a return on your investment and on that which you are letting me use.

Lord, if you cannot at present trust me with success, if you know that I might grab my blessings and rush off in the opposite direction from you, then Lord, humble me and help me to become fit and trustworthy to advance in my career for your honor.

In Jesus' name I pray.

Prayer for Safety

Dear Lord:

Your word reminds us that ". . . safety is of the Lord,"[10] so I come asking for it.

> [If your need is deliverance in a specific hazardous situation, or just in general at all times, state what you are asking for.]

I pray that my car [or gun, tool, golf club, etc.] may never be a source of injury to another. According to your will, deliver me from accident and injury. Give me judgment and skill in my actions [driving, flying, walking, swimming, or whatever].

---

[10]Pr. 21:31.

I thank you for what you deliver me from that I may never know or recognize.[11] I thank you that if I am in the center of your will I am in the safest place in the world.

I rejoice that except by your permissive will, powder can't blow me up, fire can't burn me, water can't drown me. I know that you have promised that if you do permit occurrences that seem unfortunate, it will be for a profitable purpose, and that you will be with me in the experience.[12]

I thank you, Father, that you are on watch twenty-four hours a day,[13] therefore I can ". . . both lay me down in peace, and sleep; for thou, Lord, only makest me dwell in safety."[14]

In Jesus' name I pray.

Prayer for Financial Help

Dear Lord:

Please throw the searchlight of your spirit on this crisis and reveal to me whether it is the result of extravagance, waste, or covetousness on my part. Show me whether I am failing to distinguish between needs and wants, luxuries and necessities. Convict me whether my present dilemma is the result of undisciplined spending, unwise investment, striving for status, or robbing God.[15] If I be guilty of any of these sins, help me to acknowledge it, repent of it, and confess it. . . .

---

[11]Ps. 91.   [12]Isa. 43:2; 1 Cor. 10:13.   [13]Ps. 121.   [14]Ps. 4:8.
[15]Mal. 3:8-10.

[Report in full the nature of your emergency, how it came about, what the need is, the threat or disaster that seems imminent, what help you need, etc.]

Now Lord, show me how to proceed, because if I am to blame for it, even though I repent, nevertheless the consequences of my folly may still be with me. Or if the difficulty isn't of my making or due to my mismanagement, I still need help in coping with the crisis.

Show me anything I can do myself. Remind me of possible resources or methods by which to meet this need. Give me faith to believe that you can provide the solution, ease the pressure, or support me through it, as you see best. Help me to trust your promise, "But my God shall supply all your need according to his riches in glory by Christ Jesus."[16]

In Jesus' name I pray.

Prayer for Matters of Health

Dear Lord:

I thank you that I am so wonderfully made, and for the service my body has given since birth until now. Today I come to you regarding. . . .

[Fill in your symptoms complaints, ailment, need, or possible ordeal such as surgery, etc.]

---

[16]Phil. 4:19.

Father, I know it is within your power to heal through medical means or without them. It will be your power that does it in either case. Give me direction as to whether I am to consult a physician or depend solely on you, whether I am to try remedies at hand or seek prescription of other medications or treatments. In any event, may I get out of my experience whatever you have in it for me. May I be a worthy witness for you whether in sickness or pain, at home or in a hospital.

Father, because healing must come from you, whether with means or without, I remind you of the Scripture, ". . . who healeth all thy diseases"[17] and the promise, "But unto you that fear my name shall the Sun of righteousness arise with healing in his wings . . ."[18]

Lord, if you have had to put me on my back to get me to look up, deal with me and show me what I should do about it, then give me grace to do it. Or if it is not your time for it, or if you dare not heal me now, help me to accept, as did Paul, that your grace is sufficient for me[19] Also, God, enable me in my ill health, not to work a hardship on those around me. Help me to be gracious, not gruff. Help me not to add to their stress by melancholy or criticism. Strengthen them for their extra responsibilities.

Lord, give me the attitude of Job: "Though he slay me yet will I trust in him . . ."[20]

In Jesus' name I pray.

---

[17]Ps. 103:3.   [18]Mal. 4:2.   [19]2 Cor. 11:9.   [20]Job 13:15.

Prayer for Parental Wisdom and Grace

Dear Lord:

As a heavenly Father you can understand the tense situation between our child and us. You can see our goals and also our blunders in trying to help him. You can see his viewpoint and his lack of discernment. We need your help badly. This is the way it seems to me. . . .

[Spell out your fears, objectives, and frustrations in regard to your offspring.]

Heavenly Father, remind me of those times and ways I have grieved you as he is grieving me. Show me where I am lacking in love and patience and comprehension of his viewpoint. Show me where I need to back up and admit error, take a new approach, or explain in another way. Help me to have proper perspective and be consistent. You have said, "Train up a child in the way he should go . . ."[21] and ". . . Ye fathers provoke not your children to wrath: but bring them up in the nurture and admonition of the Lord."[22] Help me to do that.

Give me the words to say, your tone of voice in saying them, the tenderness your eyes would express, the gentleness your firmness would have. Don't let concern for my convenience, or my ambitions, or my image as a parent, complicate the situation. Don't let any of us be Satan's tool.

---

[21]Pr. 22:6.   [22]Eph. 6:4.

Let the child's development and your approval
be all that matters.

Thank you for helping me in this situation.
In Jesus' name I pray.

Prayer in Time of Disaster

Dear Lord:

You have said to . . . "pray one for another . . ."[23] I come to you in my helplessness
to do anything about. . . .

> [Fill in those details that identify what you
> are praying about.]

I want to go on record by means of prayer
that I am not indifferent to the plight of the
people involved. I pray for those who have been
injured and are suffering. I pray for any who
have been bereaved, for those who have lost
property or been displaced from their homes,
those without food, clothing, shelter, medical
attention, etc.

I pray, too, for any who may be trying to render assistance [doctors, pilots, radio or telephone
operators, etc.] Give them the physical strength,
skill, wisdom, or whatever they need to be of
service. Maintain their health. Provide their needs.
Coordinate efforts for assistance and alleviation.

Dear God, grant that all involved may get
from the experience whatever you have in it for

---

[23]Jas. 5:16.

them. May they be moved toward and not away from you by their troubles.

Father, if there is something I can do in addition to praying, make me aware of what it is and make me willing to do it.

In Jesus' name I pray.

Prayer for Governments

Holy and Righteous God:

We are part of a wicked nation. Corruption, injustice, lying, embezzlement, bloodshed, and the whole range of evil practices and immoral standards characterize us. We acknowledge that our guilt is beyond delineation and that we deserve nothing but penalty at your hand, but, O God, have mercy on us! Pressure us to repentance and confession that we may be forgiven and turned to ways of righteousness.

You have promised, "If my people, which are called by my name, shall humble themselves, and pray, and seek my face, and turn from their wicked ways; then will I hear from heaven, and will forgive their sin, and will heal their land."[24]

Ruler of all the earth, you have told us to pray for those in authority, and I have no right to complain of them until after I have prayed for them. Therefore I come to you about this:

> [If there is a political scandal, a local governmental crisis, an election or referendum to be held, lay it out before the Lord.

---

[24] Chr. 7:14.

quest about it. Intercede for officials who
are trying to do right but who are being
pressured to do wrong.]

Lord, show me whatever I should be doing
about this in addition to praying. Help me to be a
concerned and responsible citizen.

In Jesus' name I pray.

Prayer for Christlike Attitudes and Reactions

Dear Lord:

I have a problem with myself. It's this way. . . .

[Fill in your situation, the thing that has
hurt or annoyed you, the person who has
angered you or whom you resent or against
whom you cherish ill-will, or whatever it is
that keeps you from having the "mind
which was also in Christ Jesus."[25]]

Father, I know that the emotions I am having
are contrary to your word, but I can't eliminate
them by my own efforts. In fact, I may even
want to hold onto them. I'll first of all have to be
made willing to be relieved of them. Bring me
to acknowledgement that hate and unlove are
synonyms, and that "whosoever hateth his brother is a murderer. . . ."[26] Refresh my mind on
the way Christ reacted to mistreatment.

Lord, help me to realize that my feelings are

---

[25]Phil. 2:5.   [26]1 Jn. 3:15.

doing me more harm than the one against whom they're directed. Impress me that in harboring them I do myself a disservice, that I may even undermine my health by such emotions. Also convict me of how I sin against you in diobedience to your word, in violation of your Spirit, in reproach to your name. "Create in me a clean heart, O God; and renew a right spirit wthin me."[27]

In Jesus' name I pray.

Prayer About a Tense Situation

Dear Lord:

You know the predicament I'm in and how it doesn't seem to me to be one of my own making. . . .

> [Outline to God what is disturbing and baffling you so that you do not know what to do or how to handle the persons involved.]

Father, I ask you to enable me to be as "wise as a serpent, and harmless as a dove."[28] Help me to get your viewpoint and react in your Spirit. Give me the willingness and grace to accept humiliation or insult, if need be, rather than add to another's tensions or put an ache in his heart, or rob him of his joy.

Lord, that is high ground that I cannot reach in my own will and strength. You will have to elevate me to it, but I want this problem resolved in such a way that Satan can't use it as a

---

[27]Ps. 51:10.   [28]Matt. 10:16.

launching pad for shooting his damaging missiles. I want it to be worked out in such a manner that everyone shines instead of whines, and grows instead of groans.

Enable me to listen to the Spirit's counsel and copy Christ's example. You have said, "Be at peace with everyone just as much as possible."[29] Help me to live peaceably with [fill in relevant name].

In Jesus' name I pray.

Prayer for Travelers or Vacationers

Dear Lord:

I come to you just now on behalf of. . . .
[Fill in name and circumstances]

I desire journeying mercies for him, that he might be delivered from accidents and injuries, that he might not contract diseases or infections, that he would use his body wisely and not be intemperate in food, drink, exercise, or sleep. May he be relaxed and refreshed by his change of pace and environment.

[If he is not a child of God you might pray as follows:]

I pray that he might be drawn to you by some experience of someone's witnessing.

[Or if a child of God, then you might pray:]

I pray that he might be drawn even closer to

---

[29]Rom. 12:18, TLB.

you through some experience, that he will not be a stumbling block or bring reproach on your name by the places he goes, the pastimes he pursues, or his use of the Lord's day. May he observe your admonition, "And whatever you do or say, let it be as a representative of the Lord Jesus, and come with him into the presence of God the Father to give him your thanks."[30]

May he be on your schedule and itinerary, where you want him, when you want him there. When he returns, may he bring back testimonies of blessings to share with those who have remained at home.

In Jesus' name I pray.

Prayer for Pastor, Missionary, or Other Servant of God

Dear Lord:

Thy servant [fill in name] is sure to need your help today. I come on his behalf asking for. . . .

[If you are aware of a particular need such as protection amidst an epidemic, or power on a certain project, or wisdom for a difficult decision, ask the Lord for it in your own words. Or the Spirit may impress you to intercede for his physical strength, mental sharpness, emotional poise, social graciousness, material resources, spiritual fortitude or other need.]

---

[30]Col. 3:17, TLB.

Lord, you have told us, ". . . pray one for another . . . the effectual fervent prayer of a righteous man availeth much."[31]

Father, I rejoice that you can do more than we can think or imagine, and that it is true that sometimes before we call upon you, you answer.

In Jesus' name I pray.

Special suggestions about praying for missionaries:

Many Christians have a specific time for praying for missionaries by name, such as incorporating the prayer in their breakfast grace. Others pray for a different need on each day of the week, as physical on Monday, emotional on Tuesday, mental on Wednesday, recreational on Thursday, financial on Friday, interpersonal (relations with other persons) on Saturday, and spiritual on Sunday.

Some churches have a prayer list of their missionaries, suggesting a different one for prayer each day of the week or month. If their birth dates are available, you may want to remember each one especially on his birthday. Some Christians use a map of the world, and pray for all their missionary friends in a certain country or continent each day: African countries on Monday, the Orient on Tuesday, home missions on Wednesday, South American lands on Thursday, and so on through the week.

---

[31]Jas. 5:15.